ROBIN HOOD:
THE LEGACY OF A
FOLK HERO

Robin Hood:
The Legacy of a Folk Hero

Robert White

Table of Contents

About the World Wide Robin Hood Society 1

introduction 3

50 Robin Hood Facts................................. 5

Man or Myth?...................................... 24

'A Robin By Any Other Name' 29

A Tale of Two Counties! 33

The Dark Side!...................................... 36

Kirklees Priory 39

The Enduring Legacy 41

Little John 44

The Lost Treasures 50

Robin Hood: On Screen and in the Movies.......... 56

The Spoof 66

Fake News! 69

Nottingham Castle – "The Imposters"................ 72

Richard III and Robin Hood:- Man and Myth Personified... 75

Robin Hood In Space And Fantasy !.................... 79

Robin Hood's Day................................... 83

Rockin' Robin.. 85

Robin The Entrepreneur!........................... 91

Robin-Upon-Thames! 94

Don't Mess With The Sheriff....................... 96

The Green Man....................................... 98

Sherwood Forest 100

Sherwood Forest… Texas! 105

Social Justice 108

A Feather In The Cap 112

National Treasures! 116

Style Icon? 119

Christmas Robins! 121

Recommended Reading 127

"Lythe and listin gentilmen
That be of frebore blode
I shall you tel of a gode yeman
His name was Robyn Hode"

- A Gest of Robyn Hode, c.1450

ABOUT THE WORLD WIDE ROBIN HOOD SOCIETY

The World Wide Robin Hood Society is an internet-based organisation that globally promotes the Robin Hood legend and its associations with Nottingham and Sherwood Forest. It is **not** a re-enactment group.

Founded in 1998 by a group of marketing, promotional and information technology professionals, it has developed one of the leading Robin Hood related websites that is used extensively by the UK and international media. The Society handles press and media enquiries; assists film and television production companies and co-ordinates research and requests for information from the travel and tourism industry, students and academics and individual visitors and enthusiasts. It provides a diverse information resource on "all things Robin Hood" and the extensively used website averages around 1000 visits every day.

The organisation also maintains an established network of knowledgeable contacts and links with many Robin Hood related interests including: - the legend and its historical and academic associations; places of interest and tourist attractions; movies, television, documentary, DVD and computer game productions; literary, artistic, musical and dramatic connections; collectables and miscellaneous trivia; talks, guided tours and re-enactment groups.

The Society has successfully campaigned along with other pressure groups on numerous Robin Hood related issues and also lent its support to various good causes and promotional initiatives. It was a member of Nottingham City Council's Castle Working Group and is currently represented on the Robin Hood Marketing Liaison Group. To help fund its activities, the Society seeks sponsorship where appropriate and also operates an on-line shop stocking gifts and souvenirs.

The Society is part of Robin Hood Limited, a not-for-profit organisation who have a registered office at Sherwood Business Centre, 616A, Mansfield Road, Sherwood, Nottingham, NG5 2GA Tel:(0115) 9245434 or e-mail info@robinhood.info or visit the Society website www.robinhood.info

INTRODUCTION

If you thought you knew about Robin Hood....then think again!

Many tales have been told about Robin Hood and his traditional story of good versus evil and his quest to regain his rightful inheritance is universally appealing to all age groups. The legend has intrigued generation after generation and everyone has their own personal vision of Robin Hood - a swashbuckling hero; a romantic outlaw; a bandit thief; a fighter of injustice or a benevolent champion of the people. Numerous books have been written by historians trying to un-tangle the myth, establish his actual existence and speculate on just who he might have actually been?

In differing ways, the traditional tales of the Robin Hood legend often impact on a diverse spectrum of information and creative arts, ranging from historically related facts to various aspects of contemporary popular culture. Consequently, the subject of the globally renowned hero of English folklore has become extensively complex but the observations included in this publication should provide a brief overview of some of the key facts, issues and perceptions surrounding Robin Hood.

'Robin Hood: The Legacy of a Folk Hero' gives a brief, fascinating insight into numerous aspects of one of the world's, most enduring and iconic legends. The title discusses interesting facts and titbits surrounding the outlaw, and then reflects on how the Sherwood Forest hero has become a global phenomenon who, over 800 years, evolved into "the people's champion"- establishing Robin Hood as a powerful, iconic "brand" who played a pivotal role in the growth of contemporary popular culture.

So be prepared to embark on an interesting journey from the legend's mystical roots to how, across the ages, the tales of Robin and his merry men developed in many diverse ways that still impact on the 21st century world of today.

Whatever your opinions and beliefs, this title will reveal just why Robin Hood has become so much more than simply a mythical outlaw of English folklore.

Robert White –
Chairman, World Wide Robin Hood Society

50 ROBIN HOOD FACTS

1.   There is NO undisputed historical evidence available that can conclusively prove Robin Hood ever existed or who he really was. However, with the unlikely prospect of a 'Richard III moment' and the discovery of a DNA linked skeleton, it probably no longer really matters, because, over the centuries, fiction has triumphed over fact and the Sherwood Forest outlaw has become a global icon of popular culture.

2.   Tales of Robin Hood have been in existence since his early suggested associations with the Pagan beliefs of the mystical Green Man of the Forest and across the decades, generations have established him as the quintessential people's hero of English folklore, resulting in his present-day status as a self-promoting legend with international recognition.

3.   The malleability of the story is reflected in Robin Hood himself, who is not much more than a gathering of qualities – some of them contradictory. By the character's very 'sketchiness'- he is a man well fitted for the fluid possibilities of his adventures that allows his interpreters, or the audience, much scope for their own involvement. Robin Hood has changed so much and so often since the Middle Ages that there seems to be no one element common to his make-up. In other words, over a period of more than 700 years the Robin Hood tales have constantly been in a state of flux. The steady flow of books and films etc. demonstrates not only the legend's continuing appeal throughout the world but also its astonishing amenability to fresh interpretation.' *(Kevin Carpenter, academic and author of 'The Robin Hood Encyclopaedia')*

4.   Like it or not, the Nottingham city and county local authorities are inseparably linked to the Robin Hood legend and have no choice in the matter. They cannot 'cherry-pick' the mixed blessings that the traditional historical associations bring and have to accept the world famous links at face value – warts and all! As a result, the authorities have often been accused of seemingly 'getting on the Robin Hood roundabout' when it conveniently suits them and in the eyes of the outside world they are often viewed as having scant regard for the potential economic benefits of the legend, paying it little more than 'lip service'. Past experience has also shown the Robin Hood connection with Nottingham and Nottinghamshire to be 'both a blessing and a curse' - generating both positive and negative coverage. However, despite being seen as somewhat unpredictable, the subject of Robin Hood never fails to spark interest and controversy in the local, national and global media.

5.   Many   worthwhile,   charity-based initiatives have been founded on the popular principles of the legend by organisations that have recognised the high profile that the Robin Hood connection generates in terms of publicity and awareness relating to 'robbing the rich to give to the poor' and fighting for causes against injustice. Two prominent examples are the Robin Hood Foundation, which cares for the needy and the homeless in New York City and the Oxfam co-ordinated Robin Hood Tax campaign lobbying for a core fund to be created to help tackle global famine and humanitarian crises.

6.   The Robin Hood legend impacts on so many areas of interest and popular culture that the World Wide Robin Hood Society have had to create 22 specific categories in their archives and on their website. They cover Robin Hood in history and legend; in business and commerce; in the community; in spirit and religion; on location; in education; in food and drink; in popular culture; in literature; in poetry and verse; on stage and screen; in music; in art; in humour; in science fiction; in ecology; in sport and pastimes; in principle; in tourism; in marketing; in the media and in the 21st Century. All of which reflects the sheer complexity and scope of the iconic legend and why it has continued to intrigue and fascinate generation after generation.

7.   One of the greatest assets of the Robin Hood legend is its ability for the story to be constantly re-told and 're-invented' in numerous ways, ensuring that Robin Hood remains a topical and iconic figure that is frequently featured in media stories around the globe.

8.   'Robin lived at some time between 1250 and 1350 during the reigns of the first three Edwards.' claimed author and historian, Jim Bradbury in his 2002 comprehensive analysis of the historical evidence available on Robin Hood. According to Professor Bradbury, 'He was outlawed and pursued a criminal career. He operated first in Yorkshire and then in Sherwood and Nottingham – probably with survival as his main aim. So far as we know, he had nothing to do with the Crusades, had no love called Marian, was not an enemy of Prince John or a friend of King Richard and was not especially caring about the poor!' This of course only represents one specific view on the legendary outlaw and the Society's research to date clearly shows there are well over 25 names and plausible theories put forward by historians and academics claiming the possible origins of exactly who Robin Hood really was!

9.   In terms of his heritage and legendary status, Robin Hood has become a million times richer as a global icon of popular culture than as a genuine historical figure. The motion picture industry has always recognised the visual appeal of the Robin Hood legend from the very first critically acclaimed silent film starring Douglas Fairbanks, to a host of classic box office blockbusters through the subsequent decades and at the time of writing this title we are aware of several Robin Hood-related Hollywood movies currently in various stages of production. Each year, many new books also generally get published reflecting the Robin Hood story in various different genres.

10.   Walt Disney had a personal fascination with the Robin Hood legend, which is why he made both live action and animated versions of the tale, as well as comedy shorts featuring some of his popular cartoon characters. He believed that marketing his fantasy creations as if they were 'real' individuals or bona fide commercial products was the key to their successful and lasting popularity and history has proved his theory to be right!

11.   He is a national folk-hero and also a symbol transcending international boundaries.

As a peasant hero Robin has come to symbolise justice, freedom from oppression and the struggle against tyranny in all its forms. It is this symbolism that is perhaps most significant, the sense that the actions of the common man are worthy, and on occasion, able to influence the course of human events. It seems fitting, then, that although the tales of Robin Hood have developed a vibrant life of their own, upon investigation the legend itself seems to be firmly rooted in history.'
(Dan Shadrake, Britannia battle re-enactment society)

12.   Over the years, the amount of paper used in the numerous Robin Hood related consultations, feasibility studies and reviews commissioned by the various local authorities probably accounts for more trees than currently exist in the present-day Sherwood Forest! Even more alarming is the fact that the collective cost of all these fruitless paper exercises could possibly have financed the creation of a quality Robin Hood visitor attraction several times over! The list of failed ventures includes the Tales of Robin Hood and the World of Robin Hood visitor attractions together with numerous medieval village style proposals. The reasons for their eventual demise varied from lack of investment to wrong location and several proposed schemes only used the Robin Hood connection to help secure property developments and showed no long term commitment to the legend.

13.   'We're a bit like a band that refuses to play its biggest hit!' was how Nottingham City Councillor, Nick McDonald responded to the frequent criticism of the local authorities by the public and the media for failing to fully capitalise on the potential economic benefits of the global appeal of the Robin Hood legend. In fact, in 2004, the BBC Television's

'Inside Out' programme filmed a feature that highlighted just how little there actually was for visitors to Nottingham to see about Robin Hood!

14. **"There has been a feeling for as long as I can remember that Nottingham has underused and undersold one of its greatest assets."** In the past, attempts to promote Robin Hood have been regarded as flimsy and lightweight and it needs something to really hold the public's imagination.' *(Ted Cantle, Chairman of the Nottingham Castle Trust.)*

15. **'I was highly excited walking up to the gate but once through, it was 'HUH!' To my dismay, the guard told me that the Castle got destroyed during the Civil War in the 1600's. I was despondent!'** These were the observations of David Miller from the Utah Desert, USA after bringing his family all the way to Nottingham to experience at first hand a fascination with the legend of Robin Hood that he had passionately held since his childhood!

16. **Although it was well known that the Robin Hood legend was popular all around the globe, it was only with the development of the internet that the true extent of its international appeal became apparent.** When the name 'Robin Hood' was typed into Google on 2nd June, 2015, the search engine came up with 66,700,000 results! When all the other key characters and locations associated with the traditional tales were also individually 'Googled' and added, the Robin Hood legend collectively totalled a staggering 1,356,011,000 results!

17. **The most important aspect of effectively managing Nottingham and Nottinghamshire's traditional Robin Hood associations is the need**

to realistically strike an acceptable balance between its benefits and its potential difficulties. Visitor expectations need to be satisfactorily met but not to the extent of Nottingham becoming an urban version of a tacky seaside resort!

18. A wide range of companies and organisations (local, national and international) have recognised the publicity and marketing value of profiling a Robin Hood connection and have deliberately chosen a Robin Hood brand name to promote their products and services. In many cases they have no real claim or links with the legend at all but they recognise that the general public firmly believe the Robin Hood name stands for a fair and just deal and hope that by association, such principles might help establish their business or organisation to also be seen as credible and trustworthy in the public's eyes!

19. In terms of shared heritage and mythology, there is now a more proactive attempt to re-incorporate Robin Hood into the city's identity. With contemporary challenges such as widening income inequality and the social impacts of austerity, the Robin Hood legend could be seen as gaining greater relevance.' *(Chris Lawton, Senior Research Fellow, Nottingham Business School)*

20. Some historians and academics believe that the origins of the Robin Hood character are possibly derived from the mysterious and mythological 'Green Man' of the ancient medieval May Games who symbolises the fertility cycle of the natural world and the re-birth of the seasons. With the growing emphasis on eco-environmental matters, such legendary Robin Hood associations offer the potential for some powerful marketing and publicity opportunities to promote the appreciation and conservation of the Natural World and its fragility.

21. **In marketing and publicity terms the generic Robin Hood 'brand' ticks every box in the promotional textbook and is the envy of cities and locations worldwide.** However, the irony of the Robin Hood issue is that having reached the ultimate pinnacle of marketing success and become an instantly recognised established icon, over the decades, to the shock-horror of the outside world, the ability to successfully capitalise on the real potential of that enviable status seems to constantly elude the authorities!

22. **For over eight centuries the characters and principles of the popular tales have continued to fascinate and intrigue each new generation** and they still have a social relevance to many of the key global issues currently facing the world today!

23. **'I believe that before Nottinghamshire can maximise the potential of the Robin Hood legend it will be necessary to package what is known through folklore, historical records and the places associated with Robin Hood into a totality that can be marketed to a number of different markets.'** This was one of the comments made by an events company MD in response to the Society's 2015 Robin Hood Business Survey. Two other comments made to the Survey were: 'Massively under-sold as an opportunity for local businesses – particularly in retail and tourism. There needs to be a bigger sense of pride. It's all very well 'us' in the city down-playing it but visitors WANT it!' and 'Marketing specialists will always advise on capitalising on strengths. Firms pay fortunes and often fail in efforts to gain brand awareness. One of the most powerful brands in the world is Robin Hood, ranking in line with Coca Cola, MacDonald's yellow 'M' and Disney – time to wake up and smell the coffee!'

24. The late Jim Lees, was a respected local historian and author who campaigned tirelessly to try to prove that Robin Hood really did come from Nottingham. However, he always said that whenever people asked him to tell them about Robin Hood he would ask if they wanted to hear the historical truth or the legend and 9 times out of 10 they would say 'the legend!'

25. The rich heritage of place names and locations associated with Robin Hood and other members of his merry band reflects the extensive popularity of the traditional tales and how far their impact has spread around the world. Street names, hotels, inns and public houses, together with thousands of commercial business and company names are all a testimony to the phenomenal appeal of the legendary folk hero.

26. On October 9th, 1966, the then Sheriff of Nottingham, Councillor Percy Holland, actually officially pardoned Robin Hood and stated that he 'shall be welcome in the City of Nottingham at all times!'

27. The global appeal of Robin Hood and his legendary associations with Nottingham Castle and his arch-enemy the Sheriff of Nottingham continues to draw visitors to the City and Sherwood Forest 365 days a year. In fact, it is a self-promoting, un-stoppable marketing and publicity juggernaut that sadly is currently seriously under-provided for and often disappointingly fails to live up to visitor expectations. The legend has attained such a high global profile that, hypothetically speaking, if for some draconian reason the authorities were to withdraw any references to Robin Hood from the City and County's promotional and publicity material, it would doubtless have only limited impact, as Robin's fame is so firmly established in global popular culture that visitors would still continue to seek the Robin Hood experience for generations to come!

28.   Tales of Robin Hood and his exploits are thought to have been originally passed on in story and song by the travelling minstrels and troubadours of medieval times. The first literary reference to him came in 1377 in William Langland's 'Vision of William Concerning Piers Plowman'. By the start of the 15th century the first poem about the outlaw had appeared and it is believed that around the same time the 'Gest of Robyn Hode' was assembled from several earlier tales. This 13,900 word work has subsequently been published in various forms and continues to be the subject of much scholarly interest and interpretation.

29.   Even though Robin Hood and Manchester United Football Club would appear to have little in common, they are both world famous icons in their own right and ironically, they both share the same basic problem of how to get the maximum potential benefits from their respective huge global fan bases!

30.   When researching the commercial use of Robin Hood related names in the food, drink and hotel industries, an initial sweep on Google randomly revealed numerous public houses, inns, hotels, bars, restaurants and bistros etc. throughout the length and breadth of the UK, as

**well as establishments in the following
international locations:** Accra (Ghana), Bondi
Junction, Frankston and Gippsland (Australia), Bailey
Island (Maine, USA), Orange & Waverley (New South
Wales), Norwood (California, USA), Ningbo (China),
Alanya and Hisaronu (Turkey), Big Bear Lake
(California USA), Adelaide, Ballarat, Sydney and
Victoria (Australia), Cedar Falls (USA), Arnhem
(Netherlands), Aachen (Germany), Bermuda, Chicago,
Rehoboth (Delaware, USA), Laganas (Greece), Montreal
(Canada), Philadelphia (USA), Jersey, Kent (Ohio, USA),
New Jersey (USA), Washington and Van Nuys (USA),
Valley Road (Clifton, USA), Benidorm, Lloret de Mar
and Puerto de la Cruz (Spain), Paphos (Cyprus),
Bangkok, Barcelona and Benalmadena (Spain), Colorado
Springs (USA), Istanbul and Taksim (Turkey), Magaluf
and Salou (Spain), Los Angeles, Cedar Mountain (North
Carolina, USA), Sherman Oaks (California, USA), Stalis
(Crete), Thailand, Tenerife, Valencia, Zurich and
Bloomington (Illinois, USA).

**31.   According to the respected historian the
late Eric Hobsbawm, a true 'Robin Hood' must
have begun their outlaw career as a victim of
injustice and NOT as a result of committing any
actual crime.** They prove that justice is possible and
that poor men need not be humble, helpless or meek.
Professor Hobsbawm believed that the Robin Hood
legend cannot die and why the character was invented -
even when he does not really exist! 'The poor and
oppressed will always have need of him as the people's
champion, for he represents justice, without which
kingdoms are nothing!'

**32.   Many famous names have been inspired
by the Robin Hood legend and have publicly
made reference to aspects of its ideals.** These

include authors Mark Twain and John Steinbeck; the US President, Barack Obama and the late Steve Jobs, co-founder of the Apple IT empire. Movie makers Steven Spielberg and George Lucas were also childhood fans who drew inspiration from the Sherwood hero for some of their characters and plot lines, recognising that although everyone initially becomes familiar with the Robin Hood legend in their childhood, the impact and appeal of the romantic adventure tale stays with us throughout life, categorically proving that it is a misconception to assume that Robin Hood is just for kids! Stan Lee, the legendary graphic artist behind Marvel Comics recalls in his autobiography that it was seeing the Errol Flynn "Adventures of Robin Hood" film over and over again as a young boy that sparked his imagination and led to the creation of his superheroes such as the Incredible Hulk, the Amazing Spiderman, the X-Men and the Fantastic Four.

33.   Sculptor James Woodford meticulously researched the details for Nottingham's famous Robin Hood Statue and created a stocky-built figure that depicted how the historians believed medieval foresters from the period would look. The public however, were expecting an Errol Flynn type interpretation, sporting a pointed cap with a jaunty feather – so a controversial debate was born that continues even to this day, with comments still being made about Robin's headgear being an authentic, forester's leather skull cap rather than the triangular felted hat that Flynn wore!

34.   In 2004, when the former Chief Executive of Experience Nottinghamshire, Professor John Heeley, first took up his position, in a lengthy article in the Nottingham Evening Post, Business Post supplement (9/11/04) he stated in headline

quotes that 'We should build on Robin's fame to draw crowds.' Further adding that pursuing a major attraction built around the legendary hero was a 'no-brainer.' He went on to say, 'We need a major attraction, backed by private sector investment that capitalises on the legend and would give us a fantastic base on which to build short breaks. Robin Hood is known and loved worldwide and we need a 365 day a year attraction of Legoland significance that operates to the very highest standards.' Yet, ironically, within just a few months, he introduced the widely-ridiculed 'Slanty N' identity campaign and comments received in response to the Robin Hood Business Survey carried out in 2014/15 clearly implied that this embarrassing debacle still cast a long shadow over any branding issues for Nottingham and, to this day, creative marketing companies remain very wary of getting their fingers burnt!

35.   The British Library has almost two thousand Robin Hood related items catalogued in its collection. These include nearly 1000 books, together with articles, musical scores, audio works, journals, maps and theses etc.. The University of Nottingham also has a collection of Robin Hood related books in its Manuscripts and Special Collections section and the World Wide Robin Hood Society archives also holds several hundred books, articles, audio, video and graphic items, together with access to numerous examples of Robin Hood's representation in popular culture.

36.   'Robin Hood is one of the most valuable pieces of property that Nottingham has got. Not so much intrinsically but as the embodiment of an idea. He is the public relations man's dream – handed to the city on a plate, for whenever Robin Hood gets a mention Nottingham gets a hefty plug –absolutely free'. These observations were made in 1977 by veteran Nottingham Post journalist, Emrys Bryson and his statements are still valid today!

37.   Because Sherwood Forest originally stretched northwards up to Barnsdale Forest in Yorkshire, claims are often made that Robin Hood actually originated from that county and it was where many of his legendary exploits took place! In 2004, the issue reached a new level when Yorkshire MP David Hinchcliffe introduced a non-binding motion in the House of Commons, calling for the House to recognise Yorkshire's claim to the legend! Nottinghamshire MP for Bassetlaw, John Mann dismissed Yorkshire's claims as a 'historically inaccurate myth' and the long-standing popular culture references to Nottingham Castle and the Sheriff of Nottingham in the traditional, legendary tales once again blew the Yorkshire theory to pieces!

38.   'Every generation creates for itself the Robin Hood that it needs. The traditional material can be tailored to suit the times and its extraordinary adaptability adds to its widespread popularity. The vitality of the legend has the capacity to pull in the audience from the start and is an idyll that seems to appeal to deep human needs – universal and timeless!' *(Brian Alderson, Chairman of the Children's Books History Society and former editor of the London Times).*

39.   Claims that you cannot create a visitor attraction around a mythical figure like Robin Hood are totally disproved by the success of such ventures as the Sherlock Holmes Museum on Baker Street, London; the Harry Potter Experience at Elstree and Peppa Pig World, near Southampton.

40.   There are 7 supposed grave sites that claim to be the final resting place of Robin Hood but ironically, considering all the Robin Hood tourist focus that popular culture has bestowed upon Nottingham, these supposed 'graves' mostly lie overgrown and forgotten miles to the north, south and east of Nottingham city! Although each of these sites has a limited degree of plausibility, none can be supported by authentic archaeological evidence and rely for the most part on links with traditional folklore. The 8 key contenders claiming to be Robin Hood's 'burial place' are Kirklees Priory in North Yorkshire; Kirkstall Abbey, near Wakefield; Nostell Priory at Wragby, nr. Doncaster; Wakefield Cathedral Church of All Saints; Loxley churchyard, Staffordshire; Holbeck, Nottinghamshire and Crosby Ravensworth in Westmoreland.

41.   Nottinghamshire County Council recently entered into the development of a new Sherwood Forest Visitor Centre in conjunction with a consortium led by the RSPB and the £5.3m project was officially opened in 2018. Working with Thoresby Estate and The Sherwood Forest Trust, the consortium will also manage the world-famous Sherwood Forest Country Park. The county council has also stipulated that safe and free access to the Forest will be maintained by the RSPB and its consortium of partners. Located at Forest Corner, close to Edwinstowe village – the new facility provides a stunning gateway to historic Sherwood Forest, for all the local national and international visitors who come to see the natural habitat of the ancient woodlands and experience the environment famously associated with the Robin Hood legend.

42.   With the aid of a Heritage Lottery Fund grant, the Nottingham Castle Trust is currently

engaged in a £24 million refurbishment project to create a world class visitor attraction. As part of the re-development at the Castle there will be an immersive, highly interactive gallery on Robin and the Rebels targeted at families, school students aged between 8-14 and all interested Robin Hood fans. The gallery will be entertaining, memorable and thought provoking and look at the development of the Robin Hood legend, including asking where did the stories and ballads come from and finding out why, if Robin Hood didn't exist, people felt the need to invent him. As well as unpicking the stories of Robin, the outlaws, Sherwood Forest and Nottingham Castle, the gallery will also look at the development of the modern beliefs about Robin built through popular culture, especially films and television. The research for the gallery is being led by Dr Richard Gaunt, from the history department at Nottingham University together with Adrian Davies from the Nottingham Castle team. The gallery design is by Casson-Mann who are the award-winning designers for the new World War I galleries at the Imperial War Museum, London. The design for the gallery will include immersive films, multi-user interactive games, theatre as well as displays of objects and other source materials. As well as detailed research, the team is identifying objects that will form part of the core display both from the Museum's own collections and elsewhere. They are also looking at a number of episodes of rebellion connected with the Castle and Nottingham, part of their research is considering the role of Nottingham as a centre for dissent before and after the time of Robin. Work began on-site in 2018 and the project is scheduled to be completed and open in 2020.

43.   From a geographical perspective, Robin Hood is said to predominantly have 'historical' associations with locations in the six English

counties of Nottinghamshire, Yorkshire, Derbyshire, Staffordshire, Lancashire and Cumbria. However, there are also places with a Robin Hood reference in Berkshire, Cheshire, Essex, Gloucestershire, Hampshire, Herefordshire, Norfolk, Northamptonshire, Northumberland, Shropshire, Somerset, Surrey, Warwickshire and Wiltshire.

44. 'Robin Hood did not die. Like the old soldier, he simply faded away. But not from the pages of legend. Long after the colourful and blood-stained pageant of kings and princes, knights, ladies, monks and minstrels has passed on through history, who, at last has made the greatest impression on our destiny? Dare we say that the true deeds of ordinary men, of Robin Hood and his like, may in the long term, have had the greater effect on society and upon the freedom of the common people both here and abroad? Even in our modern world, the battle against ignorance, poverty and social injustice goes on and the fight for freedom seems never- ending. But men would do well to remember Robin's ancient vows of chivalry.' *(Tony Molyneux- Smith, author of 'Robin Hood and the Templars.)*

45. The 'Man or Myth' / 'History versus Fantasy' debate that surrounds the Robin Hood legend frequently creates divisive argument. However, although some sections of the academic world are critically dismissive of modern day popular culture references to the legend, they could be accused of having 'double standards', for many of the earlier historical documents they study are in reality only the written accounts and opinions created by the scribes and storytellers of the time - similar in concept to the contemporary versions and viewpoints on the legend that authors and writers continue to produce today!

46.   'Over the years, the Legend of Robin Hood has lost nothing in the telling. Indeed, it is with the telling that the legend originated; many have since placed Robin Hood under the microscope and tried to document, explain and justify him but as the Sheriff found out, he is a very slippery and elusive character!' *(Richard Rutherford-Moore, author and historical advisor.)*

47.   As the legend developed Robin Hood's personal characteristics became much harder to define and the highly respected Professor Stephen Knight, often referred to as the world's premier Robin Hood scholar, summed up the dilemma in his mythic biography by stating 'So in the twentieth century Robin, both cinema star and novelist's hero, stood sensitive cheek by sturdy jowl with a figure weighed down with facts, history, location and his own elements of wishful thinking and values.'

48.   'Whoever Robin Hood was, and whenever, precisely, he lived, he would have been as much a part of, and influenced by, the nature of his surroundings as we are today. His life cannot be separated from his 'times' because without those times there would have been no famous outlaw, only a man who lived and died largely unnoticed and who was quickly forgotten' *(David Baldwin, medieval historian and author of 'Robin Hood – The English Outlaw Unmasked')*

49.   The City of Nottingham owes an enormous debt of thanks to local businessman and benefactor, the late Phillip Clay, for his visionary gift of the Robin Hood Statue and the surrounding figures and plaques. Fortunately, over the 64 years since its original unveiling in 1952, the statue has provided the ideal photo opportunity for tourists visiting the city from home and abroad. Without Mr. Clay's generosity, what else of significance would there have been for visitors to see about Nottingham's legacy of the world's greatest outlaw!!

50.   'No English Hero can claim anything like the enduring mythic stature of the Outlaw of Sherwood. He is also the only lasting myth to arise from the high Middle Ages and the last western legend to achieve a sustained international appeal. Never again would any European figure be the centre of so truly living and vibrant a mythology!' *(Jefferey Syngman, author of 'Robin Hood: The Shaping of the Legend.)*

MAN OR MYTH?

Man or Myth? Invariably, that is the most frequently asked question about Robin Hood and because there is no conclusive, undisputed historical evidence that categorically proves his actual existence or who he really was, Robin has become an extremely divisive figure and the elusive mystery as to his true origins only adds to the intrigue and fascination. *Whether he lived or not, no longer really matters.*

Over the centuries, fiction has triumphed over fact and the tales of England's famous outlaw have become a worldwide legend establishing Robin Hood as "the People's Hero" and elevating him to "international celebrity" status as an icon of popular culture with a fan base that stretches back over 500 years!

As a retired public relations and marketing professional, my own personal interest in Robin Hood has never been about the historic "man or myth" issue but has been more practically focussed on how Nottingham's legendary figurehead evolved into a powerful global "brand" and how that phenomenal promotional potential might be more effectively harnessed for the benefit of his home city and county.

The discovery of Richard III 's remains under a Leicester car park inevitably sparked off some rival comments about the "historic credibility" of the find compared with Robin Hood's "fantasy existence". However, both characters are recognised internationally and fact or fiction should make little difference when it comes down to effectively marketing their respective appeal to the local, national and global tourism industry.

The Walt Disney Organisation attributes it's highly successful marketing mantra to being based on the fact that they treat their fantasy creations as "real commercial brands or personalities" and actively exploit every opportunity to vigorously promote their marketing and publicity potential. A glance through any of the promotional and media packs that accompanied some of their animated classic movies shows just how seriously they adopted this practice and their success proves how effective this strategy was.

Who was Robin Hood?

Robin is famous for his gallantry, robbing the rich to feed the poor and fighting against injustice and tyranny. Anyone who knows of Robin has also heard the stories of his outlaw band. The names of Little John, Friar Tuck, Maid Marion, Allan a Dale, Will Scarlet, Much the Miller and the evil Sheriff of

Nottingham are as much a part of the legend as Robin Hood himself.

The stories of Robin portray him as a fearless outlaw leading his band of "merry men" (and women) against the tyranny of Prince John, The Sheriff of Nottingham and Sir Guy of Gisbourne. A brilliant archer, Robin lived a life of adventure - poaching the King's deer from the outlaws' retreat in Sherwood Forest.

Stories about the adventures of Robin have been told and retold for over eight hundred years. However, in Robin's time, few people could read or write so consequently little was written down about the exploits of our hero. Instead, people learnt about Robin and his band through the ballad and song of wandering minstrels who weaved a patchwork of fact and fiction into the contemporary culture of the time.

When did Robin live?

Historians and researchers have a range of views placing Robin anywhere between 1190 and 1307, but generally believe that Robin Hood was alive around the thirteenth century. The earliest written reference to Robin Hood is in William Langland's poem - "The vision of William concerning Piers Plowman" which was written in 1377. The poem says:

"I do not know my paternoster perfectly as the priest sings it. But I know the rhymes of Robin Hood and Randolph, earl of Chester".

Clearly, for the Gest of Robin Hood to be compiled by 1400, the stories must have been in circulation well before that date.

Where did Robin live?

No story of Robin Hood is complete without its world famous setting, Sherwood Forest which in Robin's time covered about 100,000 acres. At the heart of the Greenwood encampment lies the famous Major Oak, the "council tree" of the outlaw band.

"Robyn hod in scherewod stod
hodud and hathud and hosut and schod
four and thuynti arows
he bar in hits hondus"

Sherwood Forest was of course home for the Kings deer which the outlaws hunted for their illegal feasts. People in Robin's time saw the forest as a dangerous place and travelled mostly in large groups for fear of ambush and robbery. To Robin and the outlaws Sherwood Forest was a place of safety from the Sheriff's, men.

Today, Sherwood Forest Country Park covers about 450 acres and attracts around 3/4 million visitors a year who flock to see the Major Oak and the Visitor Centre.

Each year in August the Forest plays host to the Robin Hood Festival where enthusiasts can recapture the spirit of Robin Hood in the beautiful surroundings of the Greenwood.

Where is Robin buried?

According to the legend, Robin journeyed to Kirklees Priory where he was eventually killed by his cousin, the prioress and Sir Roger of Doncaster.

It is at Kirklees Priory that the supposed grave of Robin Hood can still be seen to this day. However, there are 6 other locations claiming to be the outlaw's final resting place. *(see entry 40 in the 50 Robin Hood Facts listed earlier in this title).* Sadly, much of Kirklees Priory is now ruined but roughly 600 metres from the gatehouse a medieval gravestone was found bearing a partial inscription "here lies Robard Hude..."

> *"Syr Roger of Donkestere*
> *by the pryoresse he lay*
> *and there they betrayed good Robyn Hode*
> *through theyr false playe*
>
> *Cryst have mercy on his soule*
> *That dyed on the rode!*
> *For he was a good outlawe*
> *And did poor men much good"*

(The final verses from *"A gest of Robyn Hode"*)

'A Robin By Any Other Name'

O ne of the most significant factors that helps to continually keep the legend alive is the widespread number of locations and places that incorporate a reference to the outlaw in their name. The extent to which they are dotted all around the globe also indicates just how far the popularity of the Robin Hood tales has spread!

We probably take for granted the local names in Nottingham and Nottinghamshire that reflect the legend, such as Robin Hood Chase in St Ann's; Friar Lane and Maid Marian Way in the City Centre and Robin Hood Way in the Meadows. There's also a Robin Hood Street and a Robin Hood Terrace and outside the city there's a Robin Hood Avenue in Edwinstowe; Robin Hood Close in Eastwood; Robin Hood Drive in Hucknall; Robin Hood's Hills at both Oxton and Mansfield and three Robin Hood Roads in Arnold; Annesley Woodhouse and Blidworth respectively!

To further confuse the issue, there is of course Robin Hood Airport in Doncaster; Robin Hood's Bay on the North Yorkshire coast; a Robin Hood hamlet just off the M6, north of Wigan; another on the M1 near Junction 42 and a Robin Hood End in Essex. There's even a Robin Hood Crematorium in Solihull, Warwickshire – although we know that is unlikely to be where he ended his life!

There's also Robin Hood Gardens in Tower Hamlets, London – which are not actually 'gardens' at all but a 1960's style block of flats that were described as homes spread across 'streets in the sky'. Characterised by broad aerial walkways in long concrete blocks, eminent architect Richard Rogers, is currently campaigning with the construction industry to get Robin Hood Gardens listed, citing the scheme as 'the most important social housing development from the post-war era in Britain'.

However, although Nottinghamshire claims to be the outlaw's home county, Yorkshire actually has over twice as many place names and locations connected with the Robin Hood legend (28) and even Derbyshire has only two less than Notts!

But it's across the Atlantic where the competition really hots-up and in Nanaimo, British Columbia, Canada, there's a whole estate of Robin Hood related names including King Richard Drive; Scarlett Hill Road and Lincoln Green Place. While down in Alabama, on the Archers Bend estate there's a Nottingham Drive; a Loxley Lane and a Sherwood Place etc.

In fact, it seems that in America, to have a Robin Hood associated postal address is considered so desirable that it even resulted in the US Post Office putting its foot down when Nottingham Properties of Baltimore, Maryland tried to get the streets of its new town named after characters and places in the Robin Hood legend. They pointed out that it would cause a great deal of confusion because Baltimore already had a Sherwood Forest community with similar names!

On the other side of the world, down in Logan City, in Queensland, Australia, there is a place called Forestdale, which was created over thirty years ago and specifically named after and inspired by the Sherwood Forest legend. All the road names have a Robin Hood connection, including Nottingham Court; Alanadale Court; Lionheart Street; Abbots Place etc. and there's even a Greenwood Lake!

But it is not just about straight forward Robin Hood-related postal addresses, for if you also include the hundreds of geographical locations (such as Robin Hood's Bog in Northumberland; Robin Hood's Leap at Chatsworth House; Robin Hood's Howl at Kirbymoorside and Robin Hood's Barrow in Bournemouth etc.) along with the vast list of business and commercial companies, public houses, hotels and restaurants etc. that use the name, then you start to realise the sheer scale and impact of the Robin Hood 'brand' and why everyone wants a piece of the action. The very name Robin Hood is instantly recognisable all around the world, a factor that is the essential, 'holy grail' of any marketing and publicity campaign and the famous outlaw's name also brings with it a sense of trust and justice – two key principles at the very heart of the Robin Hood legend. That's why the extensive research previously carried out with the business and commercial sector, in the UK and overseas, always strongly reflected the belief that in the eyes of the general public, the Robin Hood name stands for a fair and just deal. On the basis of the legend's wide popularity, companies hoped that by incorporating a Robin Hood reference into their name, by association, such principles might help establish their business to also be seen as credible and trustworthy!

In truth, the examples mentioned here probably barely 'scratch the surface' of the actual number of places scattered throughout the UK and around the globe that acknowledge England's most famous outlaw hero with a reference to the legend in their name.

A TALE OF TWO COUNTIES!

With Nottinghamshire and Yorkshire frequently claiming Robin Hood as their own, the same old issues continue to re-appear. We know full well that there are numerous places in and around the Notts/ Yorks area with Robin Hood related names and connections –and the confusing naming of Doncaster's Robin Hood Airport was a real "kick in the teeth" for the Nottinghamshire authorities! After all, Sherwood Forest once stretched all the way up to Barnsdale and so it is hardly surprising that the outlaw's exploits extended northwards into neighbouring territories!

The plain fact is that it's not just Yorkshire who can point to locations with Robin Hood names! Staffordshire, Derbyshire, Northamptonshire, Cumbria, Cheshire, Essex, Gloucestershire, Hampshire, Hertfordshire, Lancashire, London, Norfolk, Northamptonshire, Northumberland, Shropshire, Somerset, Surrey, Warwickshire, Westmorland and Wiltshire all have places with a Robin Hood name! North, South, East and West - everywhere seems to want to get in on the act and claim a piece of the action – not forgetting of course the numerous places and locations around the world that are also named with a reference or connection to the Robin Hood legend.

Ironically, although Yorkshire's Kirklees Abbey is the most well-known of the supposed Robin Hood gravesites, when the site of the tomb was examined in the Eighteenth Century and excavated to a depth of six feet, absolutely nothing was found!

But never underestimate a Yorkshireman! They're quick to recognise the promotional value of the Robin Hood "brand" and its tourism potential and have made many previous attempts to steal Nottingham's legendary heritage, including a bid by Sheffield to capture the Sheriff of Nottingham at the World Travel Market in Earls Court, London in the 1980's. However, their biggest coup has to have been in the naming of Robin Hood Airport, near Doncaster – a shrewd, commercial move that whipped an obvious marketing opportunity from right under the noses of the Nottinghamshire local authorities!

In my 25 years as Public Relations Officer with Nottingham City Council and, since my retirement, a further 21 years as Chairman of the internet-based World Wide Robin Hood Society, I must have defended Nottingham's claims as the traditional home of the Robin Hood legend hundreds of times! With no indisputable historical evidence available to prove his actual existence, anyone and everyone can come up with a speculative theory, no matter how wild or improbable. So when the claims and counter-claims were coming in thick and fast and semi-plausible assumptions were casting doubts about Nottingham's validity as the home of the world's favourite outlaw, I would simply remind everyone that the traditional stories always refer to Nottingham Castle and the Sheriff of Nottingham! NOT Doncaster Castle or the Sheriff of Sheffield (or wherever else is claiming Robin Hood as its own) .... and that usually kills their argument stone dead!

THE DARK SIDE!

Istory has been particularly kind to the legend of
Robin Hood. Popular culture has made him a
symbolic icon of freedom and social justice, and
blessed him with a wealth of virtues and attributes
appropriately befitting his global status as a worthy
Peoples Champion!

However, if you peel away the numerous layers
of myth and fantasy that have contributed to his
international fame, you soon discover that underneath
the glossy veneer of his Lincoln Green profile lie some
very "dark" roots and unsavoury connections to violence
and evil that add a sinister edge to the origins
surrounding the familiar Robin Hood character!

Academics are quick to point out that, first and
foremost, Robin Hood was an "outlaw" and that many of
the "real life" bandits that various historians believe his
exploits may be based on, were nothing more than
merciless, murderous thieves who showed no compassion
or ethics other than for their own self preservation.
Medieval outlaw gangs such as the Bradburns in
Yorkshire and the Folvilles and Cotterels, who terrorised
Leicestershire, Derbyshire and Nottinghamshire, still
enjoyed public admiration, despite having committed
some horrendously despicable crimes. In fact, over the

centuries, many hardened criminals deliberately drew comparisons with the traditional Robin Hood legend to generate popular support and "soften" their image to gain unwarranted public sympathy!

We know Robin Hood has long been associated with the mysterious spirits of forest folklore surrounding the Pagan and Celtic gods, such as the Green Man and Herne the Hunter but there are also plausible suggestions that he may even have been a member of the Knights Templar – the heroic, soldier-monks who guarded pilgrims on their journey to the Holy Land during the Crusades and became defenders of the Holy Church and fought alongside Richard the Lionheart. When their mysterious Order was ex-communicated by the Catholic church in 1307, many Templar's fled to the forests of middle England which was already a haven for gangs of outlaws resisting the authorities. To help their inconspicuous appearance and to avoid detection as they moved from place to place, they often wore little more than the hooded attire befitting a monk – from which the words "hood" or "hoodlum" are derived and which some historians believe are the true origin of the name Robin Hood or Robin of the Hood – or even Robbing Hood!!

Cloaked in a secrecy that hung over their Order like a shadowy veil, the Templar's were also regarded suspiciously by their critics as "an esoteric brotherhood, hungry for forbidden knowledge" and considered to be "the witches next of kin" who forged links with occult groups in the Arab world and became involved in diabolic practices. The celebrated author, Sir Walter Scott believed their military-style organisation to be truly evil and he made the Templar's the villains of his classic novel, "Ivanhoe" - which also featured Robin Hood and his band of Sherwood outlaws.

In the early thirteenth century ballad, "The Geste of Robyn Hode", we get a glimpse of Robin's cruel streak when he mercilessly kills the Fifteen Foresters in cold blood to avenge his anger for them failing to pay him their due wager for a test of his archery skills.

Television historian, Michael Wood, states that by 1300, the term "Robehode" was commonly used to describe any local villain and several Hods and Hoods appear in court registers of the day with the first name Robert – including a family from Wakefield, in Yorkshire, who between 1270 and 1340, were notorious for their casual, brutal violence and anti-social behaviour and became the medieval version of modern-day "neighbours from hell" !

Even present-day criminals still aspire to likening themselves to England's Sherwood folk hero. However, fraudster, Ian Pass, must have regretted bragging "Robin Hood used a bow and arrow. I use a laptop" on ITV's Trisha Show, as it led to him being jailed for four years for deception!

KIRKLEES PRIORY

Surprisingly, Robin Hood's longest running connections with the occult and 'dark arts' focus on the many claims of supernatural sightings and vampirism that in later years have become associated with his most well-known, presumed gravesite at Kirklees Priory, in Yorkshire - where, according to the traditional tale, Robin's treacherous cousin, the Prioress, deliberately bled him to death, in league with her evil, forbidden lover, Red Roger of Doncaster.

Frequent ghostly apparitions, a succession of paranormal investigations and numerous books written on the subject, have resulted in an endless stream of media stories that have constantly fired public imagination. There are hundreds of reported sightings in and around the grave-site and probably thousands more that were not reported by people who feared they might not be believed!, Roger Williams described a typical encounter that he and a friend experienced in the 1960's, when the figure of a woman, (believed to be the evil Prioress), silently glided towards them. At a distance of five yards, they could see her face with its brooding, annoyed expression and dark, mad, staring eyes, then, without looking back, she was gone! Amazingly, this all took place at 2.30pm on a bright, sunny afternoon!

Up until the early Twentieth Century, Kirklees Park, the private home of the Armytage family, was in its prime and considered to be an area of particular scenic beauty but as the grounds and buildings on the estate fell into decline and became in need of repair, the overgrown and isolated environment surrounding the site of Robin Hood's Grave developed a more corrupt atmosphere and a spiritual 'sense of place' that over the last 50 years has evoked an abundance of supposed supernatural and paranormal associations, including claims of being cursed by vampires!

THE ENDURING LEGACY

It is over 800 years since the tales of Robin Hood first appeared in a written down format - although they had of course been passed on by word of mouth for some two centuries before that – which is an absolutely amazing length of time for such a story to survive and hold a dominant position in popular culture. So what makes the tale so fascinating that, even after eight centuries, (during which time it has been re-told thousands, if not millions of times) it can still fire the imagination of new generations and capture people's hearts? Whatever it is, the traditional story of Robin Hood and his outlaw band has got it "by the shed-load" and that's why it has acquired the iconic status of becoming a "legend"!

The essential "ingredient" that usually contributes the most towards the creation of a "legend" is having an element of mystery to the story that still remains in doubt. In the case of Robin Hood it is the question of there being no undisputed, historical proof of his actual existence. For other "legendary" characters and events, such as King Arthur's Knights of the Round Table, Joan of Arc's spiritual visions or, from more recent times, the conspiracy theories surrounding the assassination of President John F. Kennedy or the disputed suicide of actress Marilyn Monroe, it is the factor of "not knowing for sure" – which offers the opportunity for a potential "alternative" interpretation of the facts that we can all contemplate and theorise about and draw our own individual conclusions ! That is the elusive "magical" element that has the power to create a legend.

In a snapshot media-watch carried out by the World Wide Robin Hood Society in 2013, Robin Hood was constantly featured in the global media and maintained his public profile through a variety of diverse news stories and events. During that 12 month period, I personally reviewed 3 new books on the subject ("Robin Hood" an academic assessment by Professor Jim Bradbury; "The Tunnellers – Maid Marion's People" by Helen Dennis , a children's story with a science fiction twist and "The Arrow of Sherwood" by Lauren Johnson, a well-researched historical fiction novel) plus "Hood – Noble Secrets" a dramatic re-telling of the tale on an audio CD by the production company Spiteful Puppet. There were also 2 new documentaries for television and DVD - plus yet another graphic novel interpretation to add to the rich tapestry of illustrative images that continue to fascinate the fantasy art genre. In October that year, the movie "The Last of Robin Hood" starring Kevin Kline and Susan Sarandon, had its premiere, although it is actually about the actor, Errol Flynn! In March, there was controversy over claims that Robin Hood originally came from Tunbridge Wells and later in the year there were also doubts about the authenticity of a pair of boots put up for auction that were supposedly worn by Errol Flynn in the 1938 classic movie "The Adventures of Robin Hood". The University of Nottingham held an afternoon public lecture event in October at which a team of academic experts presented their thoughts on the many historical faces of Robin Hood and even the daily BBC Radio serial, "The

Archers", featured the cast putting on a Robin Hood musical play as part of the village of Ambridge's seasonal Christmas celebrations!

There was a new Robin Hood-related film in the pipeline! DreamWorks have a revisionist version of the tale in production, provisionally titled "Merry Men" which, according to their publicity, incorporated "a revenge angle that is tonally reminiscent of "The Dirty Dozen" and "Ocean's Eleven". However, at the time of writing this title, the movie is still only in the initial planning stages! In the Spring, there was a 30th Anniversary Reunion of the cast, crew and fans of the 1980's iconic HTV television series "Robin of Sherwood". There was also some controversial debate when Nottingham and Nottinghamshire's business and commercial sector was asked to "search its soul" in a hard-hitting Robin Hood Brand Awareness Survey designed to once and for all get to the root of why, in the eyes of the world, the City and County repeatedly under-exploits the potential benefits of their Robin Hood connections. All diverse examples of how the endearing legacy of the Robin Hood legend lives on!

LITTLE JOHN

Now everyone knows that Little John was Robin Hood's loyal lieutenant who was always close by the outlaw leader's side in many a classic adventure and that he was also the one who was there at the end, supporting the dying Robin when he fired his last arrow to mark his burial place. However, it turns out that in today's internet-driven world of electronic communication, Little John has been giving Robin Hood and the rest of the Merry Men a run for their money and the "gentle giant" has become quite a celebrity, discreetly building his reputation to astonishing levels.

When I typed the word "Robin Hood" into the Google search engine on the day I wrote this article, it came up with 66,700,000 results – but when I typed in "Little John", it came up with a staggering 1,210,000,000! That's over a billion more results than for Robin Hood himself! So how does Little John apparently manage to create such phenomenal global interest that puts Robin and his merry band well and truly in the shade?

There are probably several factors that account for Little John's elevated, celebrity status on Google but one of the main reasons is that, as you no doubt know, information technology search engines operate on recognising "key words" and when we look closely at the information available we find that, just as with Robin Hood, Little John's name appears in many, many different connections, spanning numerous locations and place names situated around the world, including a host of public houses, hotels, restaurants - plus an extensive range of company names in the business and commercial sector. Closer to home, the big bell in the Council House clock is also nicknamed "Little John". The results of the Google search may well have also been "skewed" by the fact that "Littlejohn" is a widely used surname (including Daily Mail columnist and controversial commentator, Richard Littlejohn) which will no doubt further add to the total number of results attributed to a "Little John" search of the internet.

We also know that there is a massive global interest in all things associated with the Robin Hood legend – not just the history and mystery of the outlaw's origins but also the vast wealth of popular culture connections embracing art, literature, film, music, sport, charitable organisations, comics and computer games etc. Wherever the Robin Hood legend gets a mention, then other key characters, like Little John, also get referred to.

But let's not steal the thunder from Little John's global popularity, because he is a likeable and much-loved character in the traditional Robin Hood story who clearly has a substantial international following of fans eager to find out more about their hero. So just what do we know about Little John and what really happened to him after the tragedy of Robin Hood's death? Well here's a brief selection of some key facts:

Mockingly named Little John or John Little because of his tall, broad stature, it is claimed that he was originally called John Nailer/Naylor because of his trade as a nail maker. Although it cannot historically be authenticated, local tradition has it that Little John's Cottage once stood somewhere along Peafield Lane between Mansfield Woodhouse and Edwinstowe in Nottinghamshire. Several theories have been put forward as to what happened to Little John after Robin Hood's death but the truth, just like the legend itself, still remains an intriguing mystery!

His "traditional" grave is reputed to be the one in St Michael's and All Angels church yard in Hathersage, Derbyshire, the village that claims to be his birthplace and to where he supposedly retired and at length died. In the Eighteenth Century the grave was opened up and several large bones were found but there was the inevitable controversy as to whether they truly belonged to Little John or, as some critics suspected, were those of an oxen? In 1929, the Ancient Order of Foresters agreed to take care of the grave and marked it with two stones bearing inscriptions. However, his eventual fate and final resting place continues to be the subject of dispute and confusion. Immediately after Robin Hood's death at Kirklees, Little John is said to have fled to Ireland to escape persecution and in his "History of the City of Dublin" John T. Gilbert records the legend of an astonishing feat of archery performed by the burly henchman in about 1189. He states that "There stands in Oxmantown Green a hill, named "Little John his shot" and he goes on to say that when the citizens of Dublin discovered him to be an excellent and powerful archer, they coaxed him to try to see how far he could shoot an arrow. Apparently he obligingly proceeded to shoot from Liffey Bridge to the hill, covering an incredible distance of some seven hundred yards!

Other accounts say that he was actually found guilty of theft in Dublin and executed at Arbour Hill. However Holinshed's "Chronicle", of which William Shakespeare made much use, claims he left Ireland and went to Moray in Scotland, where according to Scottish historian Hector Bruce, he died and was buried at Pette. Other traditions have Little John buried at Thorpe Salvin, near Worksop and Wincle in Cheshire - all facts that weave further strands into the mystery and intrigue that surrounds the global popularity of the Robin Hood legend!

Although it is unlikely that we will ever really know for sure what exactly happened to Little John after Robin Hood's death, in contrast, it prompted me to take a look at some of the various actors who had played Little John in film, television and stage productions to discover what fate or fame had in store for their careers after taking on the legendary role!

Starring alongside Richard Greene in the 165 episodes of the 1950's television series, 'The Adventures of Robin Hood', Scottish actor, Archie Duncan definitely holds the record for the number of appearances in the role of Little John! He also appeared in Walt Disney's live action movie 'The Story of Robin Hood and his Merry Men' starring Richard Todd but on this occasion he played the villain, Red Gill! The role of Little John went to James Robertson Justice, who later became well known in the role of consultant, Lancelot Hodges in the various 'Doctor' films based on Richard Gordon's series of best-selling books.

American actor, Alan Hale Sr. has the most unusual claim to fame by having played Little John in three completely different Robin Hood movies! He first played Little John as a young squire in the 1922 silent classic starring Douglas Fairbanks, Sr. He reprised the role opposite Errol Flynn in the 1938 'The Adventures of Robin Hood' and then later played an older Little John to John Derek as Robin Hood's son in the 1951 film 'Rogues of Sherwood Forest'.

Bernard Bresslaw was the then unknown actor who played Little John in the ill-fated and critically slammed 'Twang', the 1966 Robin Hood based musical by Lionel Bart that closed after just

43 performances in the West End! Fortunately for Bresslaw, he went on to become one of the regulars in the popular 'Carry On' series of films.

Clive Mantle was Little John in the HTV/Goldcrest 'Robin of Sherwood' series shown in the 1980's and he later went on to star in the BBC 'Casualty' medical drama series and more recently successfully toured with a show spotlighting the life of comedian Tommy Cooper.

Other notable actors who brought their own individual talents to the Little John role were Nicol Williamson in 'Robin and Marian' (1976); Nick Brimble in 'Robin Hood - Prince of Thieves'(1991) and Gordon Kennedy in the 2006 BBC TV Robin Hood drama series, starring Jonas Armstrong in the title role.

Canadian born, Kevin Durand was Little John in Ridley Scott's 'Robin Hood' in 2010, starring Russell Crowe. Standing at 1.98 metres, he claimed to be the tallest actor yet to take on the role and in 2018, Jamie Fox was the first black actor to play the part in Robin Hood: Origins.

THE LOST TREASURES

Mysterious tales and missing artefacts are "the stuff that legends are made of!" Strange events and puzzling disappearances all help add an element of intrigue that ensures any legendary folklore lives on – so here are some of the "lost treasures" and unexplained happenings associated with Nottingham's outlaw hero, Robin Hood.

One of the most mystifying occurrences relates to the ballad in which Robin kills the Fifteen Foresters who refused to pay him the wager that he won fairly with his archery skills and the last verse states: "They carried these foresters into fair Nottingham, as many there did know; They digged them graves in their church-yard and they buried them all in a row".

Then, according to the author and historian Joseph Ritson, the following extract appeared in the "The Star" (probably a Sheffield newspaper) on April 23rd 1796: "A few days ago, as some labourers were digging in a garden at Fox-lane, near Nottingham, they discovered six human skeletons entire, deposited in regular order side by side, supposed to be part of the fifteen foresters that were killed by Robin Hood." The

news story goes on to say that the garden stood on the
site of an ancient church that had been dedicated to St.
Michael and had been totally demolished in the
Reformation ,so no doubt the bones had been properly
buried in the churchyard. The proprietor of the garden
ordered the pit where the bodies were found to be filled
up, "being unwilling to disturb the relics of humanity and
the ashes of the dead!" The original site of St. Michael's
church and its graveyard secrets have never since been
discovered.

The location of **St Anne's Well** in the Wells
Road in Nottingham's St. Ann's district is also the site of
another buried "treasure" connected to the Robin Hood
legend. Known over the centuries as "Robynhode's Well"
- this holy well was linked to a charitable hermitage run
by the Brothers of Lazarus, who were associated with the
Knights Templar. Its spring water was believed to have
substantial healing properties and an additional
attraction was a selection of artefacts, including **Robin
Hood's bow, cap, chair, arrows, boots and
bottle.** During the 17th and 18th centuries, it was one of
the most popular tourist attractions in England and
remained so until 1825, when it had its liquor licence
withdrawn and the Robin Hood artefacts were sold at
auction to Lionel Raynor, a famous actor on the London
stage. Before moving to America, he was said to have
offered the items to the British Museum but they can find
no record. A tea room operated on the site until 1855
and when the buildings at the well site were subsequently
demolished, the town council commissioned a gothic
style ornamental monument to mark the spot but in 1887
it was taken down by the Great Northern Railway to
accommodate the 30ft deep foundations of an essential
bridge. In 1987, local historian David Greenwood sank a
shaft behind "The Gardeners" public house which had
been built at the site and confirmed that the well was still

there, saying "It's a treasure trove waiting for the next person with the nerve and the money to fully excavate it."

Another local story that claims to have located **Robin Hood's Hideout** is highlighted in actor Sir Bernard Miles 1979 book about the outlaw hero. In the epilogue, he refers to an incident in the 1820's when, somewhere near Bolsover in Derbyshire, two pitmen were sinking a shaft for a new coalmine when the earth alongside them fell away revealing a yawning gap through which there was a fireplace full of wood ash, cooking pots and utensils, blacksmiths tools and a storeroom with sacks and barrels. Against one wall was a rack of bows, broadswords and quivers full of arrows and at the end of one of the galleries was a tiny chapel with a cross still on the altar. The miners then found a skeleton wrapped in an old woollen habit, lying at the base of a flat wall with one hand holding a crucifix and the other a chisel. A long list of names was roughly scratched on the cavern wall and painfully scored at the bottom was, "I was the last – Michael Tuck." The skeleton was supposedly Friar Tuck's who appeared to have just managed to crawl there and scratch these few words before he collapsed and died. As the two miners climbed out of the shaft they had cut, to tell the world about what they had found, it triggered a huge rock fall that totally buried everything under hundreds of tons of stone and the story of their amazing discovery became just another local legend! However, Sir Bernard claimed that Robin's cave is still there, only a little way below the ground, close to one of the worked-out pits and that "one fine day it will be found again!"

For many years, local historian and Robin Hood enthusiast, Jim Lees, worked tirelessly to prove that the legendary outlaw was born in Nottingham and believed that a **lost ancient manuscript** was the missing link in the quest. The authentic, historical document was said to record a court appearance by Robert de Kyme, a nobleman born in what is now known as Bilborough and actually referred to him as Robin Hood. Mr Lees stated that the ancient court record was the most conclusive piece of evidence in existence that proved that "Robin Hood was real, that he was a local man and that Robin Hood was only a nickname." He said that Robert de Kyme was well documented in local archives and he was 99% certain that de Kyme and Robin Hood were one and the same, as their lives ran virtually parallel. The missing document was believed to be in the possession of a former research scholar who had previously been at the University of Nottingham and who they only knew as a Mr. McJohnson. Having failed on numerous occasions to track down the elusive academic - with the technological birth of the internet, Mr Lees enlisted the help of his nephew, Robert Henshaw and put out a global appeal to try to make contact with Mr. McJohnson and hopefully trace the whereabouts of the vital document that he believed held the key to historically proving that Robin Hood really had existed and was born in Nottingham. However, the task proved to be the proverbial "needle in a haystack" and to-date, neither Mr. McJohnson, or the ancient manuscript have ever come to light!

Local tradition has it that **Little John's Cottage** was once situated on Peafield Lane, between Mansfield Woodhouse and Edwinstowe, near the site of the old Roman Road but its precise location cannot be authenticated. Mockingly called Little John because of his tall, heavy stature, he was in fact John Nailer (Naylor), a nail maker originally called John of the Little. After Robin Hood's death at Kirklees Abbey in Yorkshire, Little John returned to the village of

Cromwell, near Newark where he was said to have been given lands by Alan-a-Dale. His grave however, is in Hathersage in Derbyshire in the churchyard of St Michael's and All Angel's but his trusty **Longbow** is another of those "lost treasures" of the Robin Hood legend that seems to have disappeared! The 6' 7" bow was made of spliced yew, tipped with horn and needed a pull of 160 pounds to draw it. Originally brought to Cannon Hall, near Barnsley in 1729 it apparently hung on display there until the late 1960's, when on the death of the last owner of the hall, a Mrs Elizabeth Frazer it was given to the Wakefield Museum. However, Mrs. Frazer's son later took it to a manor house in Scotland where he died in 2004 and the current whereabouts of the bow remain a mystery.

When, in 2009, author Richard Maynard published his book "Wolfstrike: the Chronicles of Robyn Hode" he added another twist to the legend by claiming in the appendix that his story was based on a bundle of old **manuscripts written by a Friar John in 1320**, that had been discovered at a Derbyshire building site in 1948, buried beneath a coffin in an abandoned family crypt. They apparently came into Maynard's possession through an inheritance from his great uncle and he undertook the translation of the original text by trying to balance the integrity of the Friar's words with a modernised dialogue. The result was an intriguing version of the Robin Hood story that leaves the reader to decide the authenticity of the author's claims - or if it was just another clever marketing ploy?

The plain facts are that **the entire Robin Hood legend is riddled with confusion** - as artefacts and stories appear in a scattering of locations all around the region and far beyond. There are villages of

Loxley or Locksley in Nottinghamshire, Yorkshire, Warwickshire and Staffordshire and an abundance of wells, woods, caves, stones, hiding places and lookouts etc. that bear Robin Hood's name stretching from Robin Hood's Bay, near Whitby to Robin Hoode Walke down in Richmond Park, Surrey? In July, 1992, the infamous Sunday Sport newspaper even claimed that Robin's body had been found buried in his beloved Sherwood Forest – supposedly clutching Maid Marian's knickers!

Everyone loves a mystery - and, from the historically significant to the weird and bizarre, a miscellany of "lost treasures", intriguing tales, strange events and places continually weave their colourful strands into the rich tapestry of Robin Hood folklore, breathing new life into the traditional stories that all help ensure that the legend lives on !

ROBIN HOOD: ON SCREEN AND IN THE MOVIES.

How film and television has played a key role in helping Robin Hood become a world-wide icon of popular culture.

When the film industry was rapidly developing in the early 1900's, seven Robin Hood films were made before 1914 – proving that movie makers were quick to realise that the legend of the Sherwood Forest outlaw hero contained all the elements for a perfect film script. The combination of history, mystery, adventure and romance made the folklore tales ideally suited to be successfully adapted for the big screen and the 1922 silent, black and white spectacular starring Douglas Fairbanks became the first film to be given a typical Hollywood premiere.

1938 saw the release of "The Adventures of Robin Hood" starring Errol Flynn, and it is regarded by many critics to be the definitive, classic Robin Hood movie. Walt Disney was also fascinated by the traditional Robin Hood tales and in 1952 he released "The Story of Robin Hood and his Merrie Men" a popular live action film starring Richard Todd and in 1973 he made a full-length animated cartoon feature with a lovable fox in the title role! Several low budget action adventure movies emerged over the decades including "Rogues of

Sherwood Forest" (1957) and "A Challenge for Robin Hood" (1962) – not to mention the numerous foreign language versions made around the globe. In 1961, Richard Greene brought his hugely successful 143 episode television portrayal to the big screen with the release of "Sword of Sherwood Forest" and Richard Lester's "Robin and Marian" (1975) depicted the ageing couple in later life, with Sean Connery and Audrey Hepburn in the title roles and Robert Shaw as the Sheriff of Nottingham.

1991 heralded the release of two big Robin Hood movies battling it out at the box office and "Robin Hood: Prince of Thieves" emerged as the cinema-going public's favourite, with its all-star cast including Kevin Costner; Morgan Freeman; Mary Elisabeth Mastrantonio; Christian Slater and the late Alan Rickman's scene stealing performance as the Sheriff! The rival "Robin Hood" movie, starring Patrick Bergin and Uma Thurman was considered by many to be a far more authentic version of the legend but it couldn't compete with the success of the Morgan Creek production – which was possibly also helped by the fact that the Bryan Adams' theme song from the movie went on to establish a record number of 16 weeks at the top of the UK singles charts! In 2010, award winning director Ridley Scott released his long-awaited "Robin Hood" movie with Russell Crowe and Cate Blanchet but although it got mainly good reviews the planned sequel did not go ahead!

Across the decades, the story and character of Robin Hood has appeared on film in many different guises and adaptations ranging from the comical cartoon antics of Bugs Bunny, Daffy Duck and Tom and Jerry to "spoof" versions of the tale, such as George Segal and Morgan Fairchild in "The Zany Adventures of Robin Hood" (1984) and Mel Brooks' hilarious "Men In Tights" (1993). Other "off-the-wall" interpretations include Robin making "guest" appearances in Monty Python's "Time Bandits" (1981) and "Shrek" (2001). Fifties cowboy hero, Roy Rogers, starred in "Robin Hood of the Pecos" and Frank Sinatra and the Rat Pack appeared in "Robin and the Seven Hoods" (1964).

The advent of television in the early 1950's gave the Robin Hood legend a new lease of life, as programme makers recognised (just like the early movie makers) that the tales of the Sherwood Forest outlaw were hugely popular with the general public and made excellent material for the small screen. The 143 half-hour episodes of "The Adventures of Robin Hood" with Richard Greene in the title role, went on to become one of the most successful television series ever. It was the idea of American producer Hannah Weinstein, who had been living in England and convinced entertainment impresario, Lew Grade that his Independent Television Company (ITC) could make the series on the basis that Official Films, an American TV distribution company, were confident they could sell it in the States. Because the concept of quick turnaround times for each episode was something new to British producers it proved to be a real learning curve. To cut down delay and speed up production they dispensed with large sets and used stock items of scenery such as a baronial fireplace, serf's hut, staircase, corridor and entrance hall which were all mounted on wheels to enable them to be rapidly moved into position. Peter Proud, the experienced British art director who worked on the series said: "We could change a whole set in six minutes! Instead of taking the camera to the set we took the set to the camera and used the same items over and over again but arranged them differently and shot them from different angles."

Numerous actors and actresses appeared in the series and later went on to greater things, including Donald Pleasance, Richard O'Sullivan, Patrick Troughton, Nicholas Parsons, Paul Eddington, Jane and

Peter Asher, Thora Hird, Sid James, Ian Bannen, Bill Owen, Irene Handl, Alfie Bass, Wilfred Brambell and Harry H. Corbett. The series was first televised in the UK on Sunday September 25th, 1955 at 5.30pm in the evening and amazingly, to this day, some 60 years later, the series is still being shown in many countries around the globe!

The series also signalled the introduction to the UK of the concept of promotional marketing, where the specific manufacture of products and promotional merchandise were linked to the popularity of the show. In the UK it was basically annuals, jigsaws, colouring books and comics, but in America, where the whole marketing exploitation had been developed, it covered an extensive range of items that carried the Robin Hood brand name including bed linen, toys and games and even hair oil! It was of course the beginning of the huge promotional marketing campaigns that today are often linked to many major film releases.

Over the following decades several other successful Robin Hood television series were created and in 1984, HTV and Goldcrest films made the hugely popular "Robin of Sherwood" series, written by Richard Carpenter and starring Michael Praed and Judi Trott as Robin and Marian. Ray Winstone, Clive Mantle, Nicholas Grace and Jason Connery all made early career appearances in the production. In 1988, Tony Robinson's "Maid Marian and Her Merrie Men" was a hugely successful television series that sent up the traditional legend and many other popular TV shows have also used a Robin Hood related sketch to raise a laugh, including Morecambe and Wise and The Muppets. Channel 5 television screened "The New Adventures of Robin Hood" in 1997" starring Matthew Porretta and Anna Galvin and in 2005, BBC Television commissioned a new Robin Hood series with young Irish actor, Jonas Armstrong in the title role and Keith Allen as the Sheriff.

Top class directors Steven Spielberg and George Lucas, along with Marvel Comics maestro, Stan Lee, have all acknowledged that the Robin Hood legend was inspirational to their work. The story of the mythical outlaw hero continues to fascinate film makers the world over and 2018 saw the release of the latest blockbuster interpretation, "Robin Hood: Origins". Starring Taron Egerton in the title role, with Eve Hewson as Maid Marian, Jamie Foxx as Little John and Tim Minchin as Friar Tuck, the film was shot in various locations throughout Europe and the producers and the Nottinghamshire tourism industry will be hoping that, once again, the global popularity of the Robin Hood legend can bring international box office success! However, hot on its heels was yet another Robin Hood movie scheduled for 2018 release, the Brimstone Films production - "Robin Hood: The Rebellion". Starring Martyn Ford and Brian Blessed - writer/director, Nicholas Winter creates a darker and more menacing edge to the traditional tales! All confirming that the magic of the Robin Hood legend continues to live on!

Inevitably, the movie and television industry's interest in Robin Hood also resulted in some fascinating anecdotes, so here's a selection of my own favourite items of trivia:

Getting carried away!

When promoting the classic 1922 silent film "The Adventures of Robin Hood", Hollywood star, Douglas Fairbanks, took press photographers onto a New York rooftop to pose with a bow and arrow and in a moment of devilment he let go of the bowstring and the arrow flew away across a few streets and through the open window of a loft where an immigrant tailor was sewing buttonholes. The arrow apparently pierced the man's backside and he ran yelping into the street where a policeman came to his aid. To settle the incident amicably cost Fairbanks $5000 in compensation!

Seeking political sanctuary!

When United States Senator McCarthy's "witch hunt" against Communism was at its height in the early 1950's, certain Hollywood scriptwriters chose European exile and wrote episodes of early ITV drama series and many scripts for the Richard Greene Robin Hood series were written this way. In 1989, British director, Phillip Saville directed the movie "Fellow Traveller" a critically acclaimed thriller that used this background to great effect. Sharply scripted by Nottingham writer, Michael Eaton, it "crackled with great one-liners" and cleverly intertwined the production of the television series with the intelligent plot.

Spectacular effects!

The original silent classic, "Robin Hood" starring Douglas Fairbanks, involved some of the largest film sets ever built. 500 workmen constructed an enormous castle by spreading out truckloads of rocks on the ground and covering them with a netting of chicken wire and plaster to make a mould for the veneer of the castle. As the walls reached higher and higher they also built a moat, a massive drawbridge (raised and lowered by a concealed petrol engine) and cavernous interiors so huge that they could only be lit by sunlight and reflectors, as in the early days of film. Thousands of costumes were designed from contemporary documents, together with swords, lances and shields. Armour, helmets and visors were made of heavy canvas and chain mail was knitted in the studio from coarse hemp and it was all covered with a stiff coat of silver paint. When viewed today, nearly 100 years later, the film may have some slow moments and some scenery-chewing performances but in 1922, before sound and colour, when presented in a three-hour show, with an intermission and a large orchestra playing the original score it must have been sensational!

Movie debut!

In the classic 1938 Errol Flynn movie, "The Adventures of Robin Hood", the young palomino horse ridden by Olivia De Haviland (Maid Marian) was in fact destined to become famous later in his movie career as Trigger, the intelligent four-legged friend of western movie and television cowboy, Roy Rogers. When 33 year-old Trigger died in 1965, Rogers couldn't face the thought of a burial, so inspired by the animals he'd seen on display in the Smithsonian Institute, he decided to have Trigger mounted with his hide stretched over a plaster likeness in a reared position on two legs and put on display at the Roy Rogers/Dale Evans museum in the city of Victorville in California's San Bernardino Valley. After the deaths of Roy and Dale, the museum moved to Branson, Missouri but its run there wasn't successful enough to survive. The museum closed and the collection was sold at auction in 2010 and Trigger went for $266,500 to the cable TV company RFD-TV.

No funny business allowed!

When Douglas Fairbanks had just completed filming his Robin Hood silent classic he was approached by his old friend and business partner, Charlie Chaplin, to see if he could use the fantastic castle set in his next film. Fairbanks asked why and Chaplin showed him. The drawbridge was lowered and Chaplin emerged from inside clad in a nightcap and gown. He yawned, strolled across the drawbridge and placed an empty milk bottle and a kitten he was carrying on the ground. He then sauntered back into the castle with the drawbridge creaking up behind him. Apparently Fairbanks collapsed with laughter but refused permission for Chaplin to use the castle as he thought it might be-little the spectacularly lavish set that was believed to have been the biggest ever constructed in Hollywood.

Counting the cost of Robin Hood costumes!
Original costumes have always been popular with movie memorabilia collectors but the values can vary significantly. In 2009, a medieval hooded tunic worn by Kevin Costner in "Robin Hood: Prince of Thieves" was only expected to fetch between £400 and £600 but when the hammer went down at the auction by Bonhams in London it sold for £3,120! The costumes worn by Morgan Freeman and Alan Rickman in the same film both went for £900 each but Brian Blessed's costume only realised £192! A dress worn by Uma Thurman in the other 1991 "Robin Hood" movie starring Patrick Bergin sold for £360 but another tunic worn by Kevin Costner in "Robin Hood: Prince of Thieves" only fetched £240!

Olympic stand-in!
Champion archer and bow maker, Howard Hill, was the marksman who skilfully made actor, Errol Flynn look good in the 1938 movie, "The Adventures of Robin Hood". In the archery tournament scene, when Flynn stepped up to the shooting area, notched an arrow, pulled back the bowstring and let the arrow fly – just out of camera range, Hill took aim and after firing one arrow into the exact centre of the target, his second arrow split the first one perfectly! Just as told in the traditional story!

Robin held to ransom!
In August 2006, when the £8m, BBC Television production of a new Robin Hood series was nearing completion, disaster struck when four vital tapes were stolen from the studios in Budapest where the series was

being edited. Eastern European gangsters were believed to have been behind the £1 million pound ransom demand for the stolen tapes, which were thought to have been taken from the studios by a Hungarian extra. The Tiger Aspect production company and the BBC issued a joint statement about the theft which stated that "Tiger Aspect had been the victim of a break-in in Hungary where Robin Hood is currently being filmed and some high-definition tapes and other equipment have been stolen. The thefts are causing inconvenience and have resulted in a delay in finalising some of the episodes. Tiger Aspect is taking all reasonable steps to recover the tapes." Although the company was believed to be insured for theft, BBC 1 Controller, Peter Fincham was furious at the huge security breach that now threatened the show! A £40,000 reward was offered for the return of the master tapes and the incident resulted in the cast being forced to re-shoot key scenes missing from episodes 5-13.

Hats off to Robin!

Probably the one item of headwear that immediately establishes an association with a single person's name is the traditional Robin Hood Hat! The familiar, triangular shaped cloth cap with a feather in it has become an iconic and recognisable item of clothing that universally links it to Robin Hood. Historians tell us that it was probably originally designed as a practical piece of medieval headgear used primarily by foresters, as its slim forward-pointing brim avoided it catching the string of their longbows when firing an arrow. The simplicity of the style, with some decorative additions, later saw the hat evolve into the mainstream fashion of the period. One of the most famous uses of the hat "brand" is by the Robin Hood Flour company who were originally based in Saskatchewan, Canada and which first introduced its stylised hat logo when the business was founded in 1909.

In fact, the flour brand became so well known as a household name in North America that the original logo actually inspired Errol Flynn's iconic hat and costume for Warner Brothers classic 1938 movie, "The Adventures of Robin Hood"!

The missing film!
In 2005, the Red Monkey Film Company were producing a documentary film about Robin Hood's links to Yorkshire and they included in their location schedule the filming of a blessing ceremony held at the gravesite that is reputed to be the outlaw's burial place in the grounds of Kirklees Priory in North Yorkshire. Although it was only a short sequence, there were rumours that Lady Armytage, the estate landowner, was apparently being particularly 'difficult' and it appears that the documentary film was never actually completed or released. Despite pressure from several different quarters, the reasons why the film never made it to the screen have always remained a mystery but according to Barbara Green of the Yorkshire Robin Hood Society , in 2007, Drew Hartley, a director/producer at Red Monkey Films stated that MI5 had somehow become involved related to concerns from the Heritage Lottery Fund that strongly promoting Yorkshire's Robin Hood connections could damage Nottinghamshire's tourist industry and lead to possible job losses ! It appears that Mr. Hartley learnt these facts from high profile executives he met while filming at the BAFTA Awards. A more probable reason for any government secret service intervention is likely to be that the Rev. David Farrant, who conducted the blessing ceremony, had a dubious reputation linked to vampirism and occult practices and there had also been speculation of a local councillor being involved. Whatever account you choose to believe, apparently Red Monkey Films continued to adamantly refuse to answer any questions about why the film was not made!

THE SPOOF

The dictionary definition of "spoof" is mild, satirical mockery and it is often said that the measure of a true "legend" is when the subject can be sent-up and ridiculed in many different ways, yet still retain its iconic status and dignity without any damage to its reputation. The Robin Hood legend is certainly an ultimate example of this that specifically proves the point - with an extensive range of humorous interpretations spanning film and television, books, magazines and political caricature etc.

Even though the traditional story and characters are often taken way outside their comfort zone, these "off-the-wall" interpretations all help widen the scope and impact of the legend and extend its influence into yet another area of popular culture – humour and comedy.

There are far too many examples to comprehensively list in the space of this brief article but here are some specific references that reflect the scope and diversity of the ways in which the Robin Hood legend has been successfully "spoofed"!

In 1993, Hollywood director and actor, the late Mel Brooks made his hilarious "Robin Hood – Men In Tights" into a hugely popular cult movie and prior to that, in 1984, there had been "The Zany Adventures of Robin Hood" with George Segal and Morgan Fairchild. There were also numerous "cameo" appearances for Robin Hood characters in such films as Terry Gilliam's "Time Bandits" and the "Shrek" blockbuster. Walt Disney's 1973 animated feature saw the popular tale re-told starring a furry fox as Robin along with a cast of lovable animals "acting" in supporting roles! However, such iconic cartoon characters as Daffy Duck, Bugs Bunny and Tom and Jerry had already played Robin in various comical adaptations and the trend still continues today, with many television cartoon series often "spoofing – up" the familiar Sherwood Forest theme!

In 1988, Tony Robinson's "Maid Marian and her Merrie Men" was also a hugely successful television series that "sent-up" the traditional legend and many popular TV shows have also used a Robin Hood "sketch" to raise a laugh, including Morecambe and Wise and the Muppets.

In the world of literature, "Robin Hood - According to Spike Milligan" was published in 1998 and some other titles that "spoofed" the story include "The Lost Diary of Robin Hood's Money Man" by Steve Barlow and Steve Skidmore; (1999); "Robin the Hoodie – an ASBO History of Britain" by Hans Christian Asbosen (2009) and a German version called "Robin Cat" by Vincent Kluwe (2008) in which the well-known characters are all feline members of a cat gang living wild and free in a modern city suburb.

Over the centuries, the Robin Hood legend has also been ideally suited for adaptation to political caricature and former UK prime ministers, Gordon Brown and David Cameron saw themselves dressed in tights and referred to as the Sheriff of Notting Hill! President Obama also used a Robin Hood analogy when addressing the nation and the Mayor of New York, Bill de Blasio based his "sketch" at the Annual Inner Circle media event on a steal-from-the-rich Robin Hood theme.

In 1991, Robin Hood was featured in the USA's iconic, satirical monthly magazine "MAD" and, in the world of spoof and satire, Robin's appearance on the cover was seen as equivalent to a celebrity being on the cover of "News Week" or "Vogue" – so perhaps that says it all!

FAKE NEWS!

With today's media headlines often being dominated by high profile cases like the Leveson phone hacking enquiry, the Jimmy Saville scandal and USA President Donald Trump's condemnation of "fake news" - we are constantly reminded that issues of mistrust, deception and speculation frequently lie at the heart of such investigations.

So it should come as no surprise to learn that, with its lack of hard evidence and abundance of unsubstantiated facts, the Robin Hood legend has been frequently subjected to numerous false claims, blatant distortions of historic events and down-right outrageous lies!

For a start, for Robin to have been active in all the contradictory periods in history that different academics suggest, he would have had to have been nearly 200 years old! Equally confusing are the literally hundreds of places around the UK with Robin Hood related names, even though there is still no undisputed proof that the outlaw hero even existed! Consequently, the legend has fascinated writers and historians for centuries and they have often let their imagination run riot and carried their interpretation and speculation "beyond reasonable doubt"!

Here are just three diverse examples that illustrate the dubious extremes into which the legend has been drawn:

American psychic and author, Barbara Lynne Devlin claimed in 1977 to have experienced being part of Robin Hood's outlaw band in one of her "regression" sessions (the process of returning to an earlier time through hypnosis and psychoanalysis). In her "other life" she claims to have become a sixteen year old girl who sought refuge in Sherwood Forest to escape the attentions of Leonard de Lacey, the Sheriff of Nottingham at the time. She became Allan-a-Dale's mistress but was killed at 19 by a pack of soldiers.

In July, 1999, academics from all over the world gathered at the University of Nottingham to discuss Robin Hood's influence on folklore, literature, geography and culture and Dr. Stephen Knight put forward a controversial paper, "The Forest Queen", that suggested the outlaw was gay! Needless to say, his views caused a stir in the international media and the subsequent publicity no doubt also significantly helped sales of his newly published book!

On 19th July 1992, the sensationalist tabloid the "Sunday Sport" carried a world exclusive, front page, headline story stating "Robin Hood Died Clutching Maid Marian's Knickers", in which it claimed that a University of Utah study group had found the outlaw's perfectly preserved body in a shallow grave in Sherwood Forest! A total pack of lies of course but the global media loved it and had a field day!

These brief examples reflect just how far the traditional Robin Hood story has been plundered and distorted in the search for "the truth" and the desire to put forward new imaginative theories to satisfy the public's insatiable fascination with the world famous hero of English folklore. Weaving its web of "truth and lies", such constant interest makes Robin Hood one of the most recognised icons of popular culture and, whether you consider Nottingham's legendary association with the outlaw to be a blessing or a curse, don't knock the fact that Robin Hood has become a powerful global "brand" with significant marketing and promotional benefits for the city and county.

NOTTINGHAM CASTLE – "THE IMPOSTERS"

As Nottingham Castle currently undergoes improvements to create an atmospheric environment that better reflects the initial expectations of visitors who generally anticipate a "medieval-style" ambiance more evocatively associated with the Robin Hood legend, I thought I would take a comparative look at a selection of castles and fortresses that have posed as "doubles" for Nottingham Castle in various Robin Hood movies and on television

They include places such as Dover Castle and Alnwick Castle in Kevin Costner and Co.'s "Robin Hood: Prince of Thieves" blockbuster; along with Chepstow Castle in the HTV/ Goldcrest "Robin of Sherwood" drama series and also not forgetting the Eastern European "castle" locations that were used in the 1996 Warner Bros. Television series "The New Adventures of Robin Hood" and the BBC TV "Robin Hood" series of 2009. All these impressive, authentic-looking buildings were, of course, often primarily chosen by location directors for their imposing facades and their proliferation of towers, turrets and crenellated battlements that all conveyed the familiar settings we had read about in the traditional Robin Hood tales.

However, if the location director could not find the ideal "castle" that he was looking for, then, in true Hollywood fashion, the movie studios would simply just build a fantasy one of their own! Possibly the greatest example of this was for the Douglas Fairbanks 1928 black and white, silent classic "Robin Hood," where Fairbanks built some of the largest sets ever seen in Hollywood and constructed an enormous version of "Nottingham Castle" (See page 61 – Spectacular Effects).

If however, location scouts want "the real thing", many consider that, with its rich history of more than 1000 years of wars and plagues, the spectacular fortress in the town of Carcassonne in Southern France represents the quintessential, authentic, medieval castle. With two defence walls, measuring nearly 2 miles long and 52 towers, it is easy to see why Kevin Costner's 1991 movie filmed many location shots inside the chateau walls. Carcassonne is a hugely popular tourist destination, where there are no entrance fees into the castle city and children are encouraged to search the atmospheric, narrow cobbled streets for the legend of Robin Hood!

In their own unique ways, each of the fore-mentioned castles reflect certain elements that have coloured public perceptions of what they imagine

Nottingham Castle to be like, based on the popular tales they have read and the film and television dramatisations of the Robin Hood legend. However, over the centuries various historical events in Nottingham's past have resulted in the site where the legendary castle reputedly once stood being presently occupied by an Italianate-style mansion, leaving the City Council and the newly-formed Castle Trust with the difficult conundrum of "squaring the circle" between the long-overdue improvements to the Castle building and also fulfilling the public expectations of visitors searching for Nottingham's traditional links to Robin Hood as an icon of popular culture. Comments in the Nottingham Post and other media indicate that it will be a challenging and somewhat complex balancing act, requiring some imaginative vision tempered with a measurable dose of reality and the inevitable compromises. So let's wish them well and hope their proposals finally bring about a satisfactory resolution to the controversial issue of Nottingham effectively getting to grips with successfully exploiting the full potential of its globally famous connections with Robin Hood.

RICHARD III AND ROBIN HOOD:- MAN AND MYTH PERSONIFIED.

The City of Leicester's success of turning the car park discovery of Richard III's skeleton into the creation of an up-and-running visitor centre in just over 2 years has inevitably drawn comparisons with Nottingham's Robin Hood focus still being reliant on a 63 year old statue! So just why has Nottingham failed to reap the benefits from its legendary Robin Hood connections? Well, as you might imagine, it is inevitably a long-running saga of myth, reality; complexity, lost opportunities, funding issues and a wavering lack of commitment – all wrapped up in endless consultants reports and hours of hollow rhetoric! Much too heady a mix for this short article, so here is my brief outline of the key issues that actually make a difference when comparing Nottingham's Robin Hood shortcomings with Leicester's Richard III success.

First and foremost is the fact that Richard III can be traced specifically to having existed as a 'real' person with a proven place in British history whereas Robin Hood's precise origins remain a mystery and the subject of much debate by historians, who all put forward various theories and contenders as to who's exploits the Sherwood outlaw might be based on. This question of 'man or myth?' has always been at the heart of the Robin Hood issue and although, across the centuries, fiction has long outgrown any true historic facts linked to the legend, when it comes down to seeking funding from the various organisations who administer that crucial grant aid, it appears that the 'mythical' factor does not apparently meet their criteria. At least this was the conclusion drawn by Focus Consultants, following initial discussions with the Heritage Lottery Fund regarding the extent to which the £24 million restoration project at Nottingham Castle might feature Robin Hood aspects!

However, although Robin Hood may not have an authentic, historical pedigree to match Richard III, he does have an un-disputed and enviable status as a defining icon in the history of Popular Culture - a history that is far richer in diversity and public interest than Richard III can ever claim and also one that stretches from the early medieval tales of the mystical Green Man of the Forest to the very latest Hollywood movies. This rich, bountiful tapestry of popular heritage has seen aspects of the Robin Hood legend embrace and influence a vast range of art and cultural genres and has also seen the principles embodied in the traditional tales have an impact on contemporary, social and moral issues.

It is the sheer scale, scope and complexity of the legendary Robin Hood enigma that makes it so difficult to get to grips with the enormous magnitude of the subject and stimulate the creative vision necessary to fully appreciate the 'the big picture'. The Society frequently receives 'cries of help' from students and researchers who, having chosen Robin Hood as the topic for their dissertation or documentary film, suddenly find themselves totally 'lost' in a network of connections to the legend that send them spinning-off, out of control in a myriad of different directions! It was this wide spectrum of associations that prompted the World Wide Robin Hood Society to completely re-format their website into 22 separate categories under the umbrella title of 'The Many Faces of Robin Hood' which, perhaps somewhat surprisingly, include references to Robin Hood in ecology, business, the community, science fiction, education, sport and spirit and religion, as well as the more obvious links to history, literature, art, stage and screen, music etc.

Robin Hood also has the power to become frequently 're-invented'- giving him the ability to remain topical with the public and the media. By comparison, the reality of Richard III's existence finds Leicester's monarch somewhat shackled to his historic roots. For while Richard's story is pretty much limited to the historical facts, characterisation by Shakespeare and the occasional play, film or book, Robin Hood gets his story constantly re-interpreted and up-dated in numerous ways and genres, ranging from contemporary social comment on the principles he is known and loved for, to teaming up with Friar Tuck as a duo of vampire killers in a poetic, Chaucer-style parody!

So, in conclusion, on balance Robin Hood would appear to have far more promotional advantages and potential economic benefits as a legend than as a 'real' person like Richard III - but the actual reality is that in the space of just over 2 years, the City of Leicester swiftly took the discovery of their 'real' king to a high profile re-interment resulting in the opening of a new visitor centre to reap the benefits of its links with the last Plantagenet monarch!

Unlike Richard III, no skeleton has ever been discovered that can be proven, undisputedly to be that of Robin Hood, so in its own unique way, the un-solved mystery surrounding Robin Hood's roots has only added to his world wide appeal and is one of the key elements that helps sustain the phenomenal, on-going interest in the legend. Whereas Richard III' s story is clearly mapped out in the pages of English History, Robin Hood's unknown, mythical origins still baffle and intrigue historians, allowing his tale to be re-told and re-invented in thousands of different adaptations and interpretations that have inspired numerous books, plays, films, operas, musicals, songs, games, locations and place names etc.

The power of mythical folklore lies in the fact that when tales are repeatedly told and passed down through the ages, over time, they become first a legend and then almost a reality. None more so than the timeless appeal of the Sherwood Forest hero Robin Hood, the People's Champion whose story has passionately captured hearts and minds all around the world and given the City and County 'free-gratis' - a priceless legacy yet to be fully exploited!

ROBIN HOOD IN SPACE AND FANTASY !

Although some historians claim that the origin of the character of Robin Hood can be traced way back to the medieval myths of spiritual storytelling and similarities with the Green Man of forest folklore, the traditional tale of the outlaw hero has also become a "time traveller" in every sense of the word and often makes appearances in the futuristic literary genre of science fiction and fantasy. True testimony as to why the ever-popular tales have established Robin Hood as a unique global legend!

Here are just a few examples of how his character and exploits have been cleverly adapted into the future worlds and fantasy realms of cult science fiction.

Even the scriptwriters for BBC's "Dr Who" couldn't resist introducing Robin into the series when in "The Robot of Sherwood" episode the Time Lord joined forces with the legendary outlaw after he had discovered that the leafy glades of Nottinghamshire's Sherwood Forest were threatened by "an evil plan from beyond the stars."

In 1991, the "Q-Pid" episode of the "Star Trek: The Next Generation" TV series saw actor Patrick Stewart get all dressed up in the traditional feathered hat etc. when the mischievous "Q" transported Captain Picard and his crew to Sherwood Forest in a Robin Hood based scenario with a romantic twist.

However, back in 1966, Canadian animators produced the first-ever Robin Hood children's cartoon series to appear on television when they launched "Rocket Robin Hood", in which all the characters and conflicts of the classic English legend were placed in a futuristic outer space setting.

In his 2006 book, "Erasmus Hobart and the Golden Arrow", local author Andrew Fish has his history - teaching hero portrayed as "probably the first time-traveller in human history" and sees him being transported into the world of Robin Hood via a home-made time machine disguised as a Medieval privy!

As part of "The Afterblight Chronicles" (a series of post-apocalyptic fiction set in a world ruled by crazed gangs and strange cults} - author Paul Kane's "Arrowhead" leans imaginatively on the Robin Hood legend against a background of recognisable Nottingham landmarks that include the Council House and Castle and action-packed imagery of archers astride overturned trams in the Old Market Square.

DC Comics "Outlaws" series also places the Robin Hood legend in a futuristic world with medieval undertones evoking a banned, "Holy Grail"- type inspirational artefact that reflects the values and principles of a long-lost, just society. In the end, the much-coveted object turns out to be an ancient leather-bound copy of the story of Robin Hood!

More recent developments of the Robin Hood character fighting for fair-play and social justice are "Red Hood and the Outlaws" – who lives by the slogan "I fought the law and I kicked its butt!" and with a voluptuous, auburn-haired, Maid Marian style female companion tries to survive in a war-torn environment riddled with military marauders.

Perhaps even more bizarre was the Robin Hood play recently presented in Williamson Park, Lancaster , where writer, Kevin Dyer depicted the legend being staged by The Dukes in a Eurozone police state with electronic tagging, klaxons and a motorbike zooming about threatening the poor. In this interpretation the writer and director had probably been reading too much George Orwell for their own good! The "merry men" in this production were all female eco-warriors including a fat lady "Tucky" and a wrestling expert, Marion! Apparently, this "mobile" adaptation also required the audience to follow the action around to six different staged venues in the park. However the critics were seemingly divided on its success; one reviewer wrote that it was "the stuff of golden childhood memories while another commented "the views out to Morecambe Bay are gorgeous, shame about the show!"

The fine line between the genres of Science Fiction, Fantasy and Horror often sees all three subjects become merged together in various interpretations and the popularity of the "vampire" and "zombie" concepts has proved to be a commercial money-spinner with the "Twilight" series of books/movies and the hit television series, "The Walking Dead."

No surprise then to find that the Robin Hood legend has also been given the horror/fantasy treatment! Released in early 2013, "Zombie Hood" was an independently produced feature film that was set in Nottingham and took its theme from the traditional Robin Hood legend. Providing the essential blend of incredulity and gore, the film was shot across the East Midlands and used a local cast and crew as well as 300 zombie extras from around the region.

If poetry and prose are more in your line, then try "Robin Hood and Friar Tuck – Zombie Killers"- in which author, Paul A. Freeman, composes 90 plus pages of rhyming verse in the style of Chaucer's Canterbury Tales. The theme describes how, while King Richard was away on his Crusades to the Holy Land, Medieval civilization became under threat from the "un-dead", when a zombie plague emerged that "used an alchemistic spell to re-animate corpses bound for Hell! The fate of all on earth – the evil and the good – was in the hands of Robin of the Hood."

For their first blockbuster graphic novel, publishers Mohawk Media and Eco Comics teamed up Robin Hood (and his Merry Women!) alongside horror heavyweights Dracula and Jekyll and Hyde to overcome a group of criminally-minded female vampires! - proving, yet again, that the Robin Hood legend has no limits to its imaginative adaptations.

Robin Hood's Day

In their quest to find the true origins of the Robin Hood legend, historians often link it to the early pagan festivals of 'Robin Hood's Day' (May 1st) and 'Midsummer's Day' (June 30th).

Celebrated to signify the arrival of Spring, a feature of the traditional event was the customary performance of a play in which a youth acting as Robin Hood would take the Queen of the May or 'Maid Marion' into the woods where the Abbot of Unreason (otherwise known as Friar Tuck) would 'bless' their coupling! The lewd and immoral content of these performances was greatly enjoyed by the common people and became the excuse for loutish behaviour and riotous feasting and drinking.

Inevitably, the authorities in England and Scotland grew increasingly concerned over the ribald tone of the celebrations and the fact that the parody of matrimony, combined with all the drink-fuelled merrymaking, gave Robin Hood's Day a notorious reputation for producing an increased number of illegitimate children born around the end of each January! Often referred to as 'the sons of

Robin', some historians claim this was how the surname Robinson may have been derived?

Even though the Scottish Parliament decreed in 1555 that ' no one should act as Robin Hood, Little John, the Abbot of Unreason or Queen of the May', it wasn't until the Puritanical influences of the 17th century that the English Parliament banned Robin Hood's Day outright. The festival was re-introduced during the Restoration period but the celebration became known as May Day and the Church and Civic authorities could finally acknowledge that they had successfully erased Robin Hood's Day from public memory!

ROCKIN' ROBIN

"**R**obin Hood, Robin Hood, riding through the glen ...." so goes the signature tune of the 143 episode ATV television series starring Richard Greene. Penned by American composer Carl Sigman in 1956, the song spent 28 weeks in the British pop music charts courtesy of versions by Gary Miller and Dick James (who later became a key publisher of hit songs by the Beatles and Elton John). When Sigman died in the year 2000, it prompted the World Wide Robin Hood Society to take a closer look at the legendary outlaw's unlikely links with the world of pop and rock music and the findings make interesting reading!!

Robin Hood is specifically mentioned in the lyrics of two UK chart hits namely Connie Francis' "Stupid Cupid" (1958) and Five Star's "Rain or Shine" (1986). Bob Dylan mentions him in his lengthy "Desolation Row" track on the "Highway 61 Re-visited" album and ELO's "Can't Get You Out Of My Head" also contains a lyrical reference. In fact band member, Jeff Lynne seemed to have a bit of a fascination with the outlaw, as he also had a song "Wild Times" included on the soundtrack of the Kevin Costner block-busting movie, "Robin Hood – Prince of Thieves", which emotively conjures up the spirit of Robin Hood and on ELO's 1974 album "Eldorado" he included a track called

"Poorboy (The Greenwood)" which makes a direct mention of Maid Marian and the outlaw way of life.

Inevitably, over the years, the musical scores from all the Robin Hood movies produced some memorable melodies, with Bryan Adams' "Everything I Do (I Do It For You)" from "Robin Hood- Prince of Thieves" holding the number one chart spot for an amazing 16 consecutive weeks in 1991, a record yet to be broken. Before then, it was the popular HTV series "Robin Of Sherwood" which put Irish folk band, Clannad, into the charts in May 1984 with their haunting "Robin (The Hooded Man)" theme tune.

However, the appeal of the legendary outlaw to songwriters wasn't confined to film and television music and such credible bands as Deep Purple and Ocean Colour Scene have all recorded different tracks called "Robin Hood". Prefab Sprout also refer to him in their song "Appetite" and the progressive acoustic band, Nickel Creek, recorded a song called Robin and Marian" on their eponymous album. The Sherwood swashbuckler also gets a mention in the MGM musical "Seven Brides For Seven Brothers", where in the song "Sobbin' Women", the brothers sing "Just remember what Robin, Robin, Robin Hood would have done..." – and in the musical version of "Chitty Chitty Bang Bang" he gets mentioned again in the lyrics to the song "My Old Bamboo".

But reference to our hero of the Greenwood does not always ensure success, as hit composer Lionel Bart discovered to his cost in 1965 when his musical adaptation of the legend, "Twang" was brutally panned by the critics and closed in London's West End after the first six weeks! However, Bart did make a reference to

Robin in the lyrics of the song "You've Got To Pick A Pocket Or Two" from his award winning musical "Oliver".

On a more bizarre note, in the early Sixties, Decca Records signed Robbie Hood and his Merry Men as recording artists and Mike West (Robbie) recalled that he wore a Lincoln Green stage outfit and his backing group had boots, feathered hats, jerkins made from sackcloth and bright red, blue or yellow tights!

In 1979, Alabama folk-rock outfit, 38 Special, put out an instrumental "B" side entitled "Robin Hood" which, in a quirky, toe-tapping way sounded like Mike Oldfield meets Guns 'N' Roses! Another Robin Hood based tune was by David Marks, (an original early member of the Beach Boys) who recorded a surfing instrumental entitled "The Sheriff of Noddingham"!

Even Abba tribute band Bjorn Again, have a clip in their TV documentary/ video which shows it's two female singers limbering up their vocal chords with a Robin Hood/ Merry Men voice exercise!

A track titled "Robin Hood" was featured by The Mekons on an album called "So Good It Hurts" and Woody Ball is listed as having cut a track called "Robin Hood and his'56 Ford" on their "Hot Rod Gang" album.

Charlotte Dahlgaard, one of the Society's members in Denmark, tells us that a song called "Robin Hood" was a Danish entry in the Eurovision Song Contest.

Another strange connection with Robin Hood and the popular music industry is that Peter Asher, who played the young Prince Arthur in an episode of the Richard Greene TV series, then went on to become one half of the duo, Peter and Gordon who topped the charts with a "World Without Love" in the mid-60's. The song was written by Lennon and McCartney and Peter's sister, actress Jane Asher, was Paul McCartney's girlfriend at the time. Peter later became a record producer in the USA and was responsible for enhancing the careers of stars like James Taylor and Linda Ronstadt.

Legendary bandleader, Louis Prima wrote and recorded a song called "Robin Hood" in 1944 that included the lyrics "They would scamper through the forest to the Blue Boar Inn" and "Had a fear for no man – only for his chick whose name was Mari-anne." Apparently Prima was such a fan of the man from Sherwood Forest that he even set up his own record label in the early 1950's and called it Robin Hood - which according to Nick Tosches, in his 1984 book "Unsung Heroes of Rock and Roll", the label produced some groundbreaking music.

"No Good Robin" was recorded in 1956 by American rockabilly artist Delbert Barker and Irish singer/songwriter, Luka Bloom wrote and recorded" Lonesome Robin". Another musical connection was made with the legend when the Clancy Brothers and Tommy Makem recorded "Brennan on the Moor" – a traditional song about Ireland's Robin Hood, highwayman William Brennan, who was tried and executed for his crimes at Clonmel in County Tipperary in 1804.

Icelandic female vocalist, Bjork recorded a single called "Robin Hood Riding Through The Glen" but, strangely enough, there was no actual reference to Robin Hood in the song!

A traditional ballad, "Robin and the Pedlar" was arranged and sung by a Mr. Verrall of Horsham, Sussex and Folk band, Steeleye Span included their version of the story in "Gamble Gold (Robin Hood)", a track on their hit album of 1975. Fred Wedlock,(a sort of West Country Billy Connolly) also has a track called "Robin Hood" on his 1981 "Village Thing" album.

According to Dr. Andrew C. Rouse, of the University of Pecs, Hungary, an artist called Keith Christmas wrote an uproariously funny spoof ballad called "Robin Head" about trafficking drugs in Sherwood and the tune is often also attributed to the previously mentioned Fred Wedlock but with the title of "Ode to Nottingham". Dr. Rouse even includes a chapter partly related to Robin Hood in his 2005 book "The Remunerated Vernacular Singer", in which he studies the relative social caste of the minstrel through text analysis!

Protest singer, Billy Bragg has a line in one of his songs that goes "Robin Hood and his Merry Men, They've all gone away. We won't see them back again."

In 2004, Bootlace Johnnie and the Ninetynines released a song on Burning Shed Records called "Down Pentonville Way" that included the lines "Now one thing my old man had understood, We could trace our roots back to Robin Hood".

The original "Gest of Robyn Hode" was probably composed in the mid-to-late 1400's and first printed in the early 16th century and is believed to be the longest ballad of its type in English literature. However, Californian musician, Bob Frank was not deterred by its lengthy verses and recorded a modern translation, full of wit and drama, in an Arlo Guthrie - style delivery that lasts for a full hour and twenty minutes !

In fact, I am always amazed at how Robin Hood's name manages to creep into all kinds and styles of songs!

ROBIN THE ENTREPRENEUR!

Although it would be hard to imagine Robin Hood swapping his traditional Lincoln Green tunic and feathered hat for a pin-stripe suit and a bowler – it's a well-documented fact that, to a greater and lesser extent, the legendary outlaw has played a significant role in thousands of business deals and marketing campaigns all around the world - and he continues to do so.

Hundreds of classic examples were identified as part of an extensive random research project carried out in 2012 that was undertaken to look at the global impact and adoption of the Robin Hood "brand" in business and commercial circles.

Ranging from high profile corporate promotions such as USA supermarket giant Wal-Mart's coast-to - coast advertising campaign (featuring their "happy face" logo wearing a Robin Hood hat and "shooting down prices") - to local, small-business female entrepreneur, Dolly Sewell's Robin Hood Greeting Cards venture that took her all over the States. From Canada's Robin Hood Flour Company to Finland's Radio Robin Hood, the global list of practical and successful applications of the Robin Hood "brand" just goes on and on!

It embraces familiar names from Nottingham's past, such as John Player's cigarettes, Home Ales and Raleigh Cycles - alongside more current examples like the Nottingham Building Society, Robin Hood Harley Davidson, Castle Rock brewery and Doncaster's Robin Hood Airport.

A particularly striking element of the research findings is the sheer diversity and creative ingenuity of many of the applications, all recognising the positive, feel-good, credibility factor that the world-renowned Robin Hood name generates with the global public - instantly creating a rapport with potential customers.

No doubt every Nottingham City and County resident will have experienced being away on holiday and, having mentioned whereabouts they are from, received the familiar response "Ah - Robin Hood!" It's an "ice-breaker" that opens a topic of conversation and represents one of the most significant and important ways in which Nottingham's Robin Hood connections have often triggered a potential business opportunity. It gives Nottingham "the edge" - a chance to "get a foot in the door", providing a springboard from which the wider business issues can be discussed and developed. There are numerous examples of how this initial breakthrough has contributed towards a successful conclusion, including the creation of the UK's first Showcase multiplex cinema; the former re-location of Central Television Studios and the N.A.A.F.I. and the HM Revenue and Customs offices at Castle Wharf.

Above everything else, the 2012 research project clearly showed that City and County were barely scratching the surface of the marketing potential of the Robin Hood "brand" and far more businesses needed to "step up to the plate" and show some creative vision. It all seemed a bit like having the whole of the Royal Philharmonic Orchestra at your disposal and only playing "Chopsticks"!

ROBIN-UPON-THAMES!

One of the most unexpected places to claim a Robin Hood connection is the Royal Borough of Kingston Upon Thames! Although it only has a population of about a sixth of the Greater Nottingham conurbation it boasts several significant references to Robin Hood. In fact a note in the minister's accounts for the year 1541 mentions the existence of a Robyn Hoode Walke in what is now Richmond Park. Even more surprising is the fact that this reference appears a full 150 years before any Robin Hood place name was ever recorded in Sherwood Forest!

Speculation suggests that Robyn Hoode Walke was named in the outlaw's honour, possibly even by the King himself, for according to local historian, Clive Whichelow, in his booklet 'The Local Mystery of Robin Hood', Richmond Park was a favourite hunting ground of King Henry VIII and the sovereign was also known to be an enthusiastic supporter of the Medieval Games that included the Robin Hood game which featured displays of archery and plays that included the characters of Robin Hood and his men dressed in Lincoln Green and also introduced Maid Marian, Little John and Friar Tuck. The legendary connection appears to have subsequently triggered several local landmarks being given a Robin Hood name and in and around Kingston you can still find a Robin Hood church; a Robin Hood Inn; a Robin Hood School; Hill; Well; Close; and Farm together with a Robin Hood Gate to Richmond Park and a Sherwood Lodge. Kingston Museum also introduced an annual Robin Hood Festival to celebrate the town's connections with the iconic legend and the event has been a great success.

DON'T MESS WITH THE SHERIFF

B efore the meteoric rise of today's instant communication networks, it was much harder for journalists to find new stories. So when, in the late 1990's, ITN News picked up on the fact that Nottingham City Council had yet to announce who was to be the next Sheriff of Nottingham, they mischievously started to speculate that the Council were planning to abolish the centuries-old office that traditionally dated back to famous links with Robin Hood.

Of course, this was totally un-true but as the Council continued to dismissively resist ITN's requests for an interview with the Leader of the Council, the news channel ratcheted -up the pressure by deciding to feature the story in their popular '...And Finally', three minute slot that always concluded their 10pm prime-time news programme.

Former Council leader, John Taylor, was furious and repeatedly dug his heels in deeper, stating he had far more important local government issues to deal with than choosing the next Sheriff! However, further telephone calls established that it was the Robin Hood connection that made the item 'worthy' of national news

96

focus and as ITN had already paid to use original footage from the 1950's Richard Greene TV series, they had absolutely no intention of dropping the story. In the end, Councillor Taylor begrudgingly listened to the advice given by the media and communication team and agreed to an interview and the resultant feature took on a more 'tongue-in-cheek' view of the issue that showed the Council in a positive light!

THE GREEN MAN

The 'Green Man' imagery is believed to date back to early medieval associations with Pagan mysticism and is often interpreted as a symbol of fertility and regeneration. Historians and folklorists have linked the evolution of the Robin Hood legend to the Green Man and to other figures from the cycle of the seasons, such as Jack in the Green, John Barleycorn, the Wild Man of the Woods and the mischievous sprite Robin Goodfellow.

Sometimes known as "Foliate Heads", the Green Man image was often carved into the decorative stonework and woodwork of ecclesiastical buildings, depicting a man's face surrounded by green foliage and often spouting leaves from the mouth. One of the finest examples of this type of sculpture can be seen in Southwell Minster, Nottinghamshire, one of the few complete buildings to survive from the time of the Norman Conquest. In the ornately decorated medieval Chapter House are a group of famous stone-carvings known as "The Leaves of Southwell" – where from amongst the scuplted foliage a number of enigmatic faces peer down.

Invading cultures added to the wealth of oral history surrounding the mythical figure of the Green

Man and the Romans, for example, introduced their gods to Celtic Britain and Cernunnos became Herne the Hunter, half-man, half-beast who supposedly haunted the depths of the forests.

Over several thousand years, stories told in the shadows of caves and around the glow of camp fires seemingly took on a reality of their own. The leafy glades of Sherwood Forest are an ideal place for such stories to grow into the globally famous legend we enjoy today, ensuring that the spirit of Robin Hood continues to live on!

SHERWOOD FOREST

The popular tales of Robin Hood's adventures in Sherwood Forest are the heart and soul of the most famous legend in English folklore. However, the Forest also has some interesting myths and legends of its own so let's take a closer look at some of the fascinating facts and superstitions that surround Sherwood Forest and its ancient oaks.

Many people wrongly assume that the world famous Major Oak in Sherwood Forest got its name because it was the biggest and most dominant tree in the forest. The truth is that it was actually named after a Major Hayman Rooke, who, on retirement from the army, moved to the area and developed a friendship with the Duke of Portland. He became very interested in the wooded landscape of the Sherwood and Welbeck estates and their spectacular trees and in 1799 he published his 'Sketch of the Ancient and Present State of Sherwood Forest'. Upon his death in 1806, as a mark of respect for the interest he had shown, the formerly known Cockpen Tree (so called because its hollow trunk had been used to rear and keep fighting cocks), was re-named 'the Major's Oak' in Rooke's honour.

The tree is reputed to have 'wintered for over 1000 years' and some claim that its hollow trunk may even have provided shelter for Robin Hood and his men, when hiding from the Sheriff of Nottingham! A pre-First World War travel guide to the Sherwood Forest area states that 'at the height of five feet, the gnarled and weather-beaten trunk measures thirty feet in circumference and its monster branches cover a straight line of two hundred and forty feet – or a circumference of nearly two hundred and seventy yards! The trunk is quite hollow to a height of over fifteen feet, accessed through a fissure and affords standing room for a dozen persons.' In fact one historian of the time recorded that 'seven persons had breakfasted together within the space and sixteen had been known to squeeze themselves within the wooden walls.'

Contemporary examination by present day botanists and tree specialists estimate that the Major Oak is most likely to actually be only 800 - 1000 years old – making it little more than an acorn at the time of Robin Hood's supposed existence! However, just like today, visitors paid no attention to such 'spoil sport' findings and Victorian and Edwardian travellers liked nothing better than to wander through Sherwood Forest's atmospheric woodland glades and re-live the Robin Hood legend in their imagination. These romantic experiences were eloquently recorded by such notable literary figures as the American writer, Washington Irving, author of 'The Legend of Sleepy Hollow', who wrote; 'As I gazed about me upon those vestiges of once 'Merrie Sherwood', the picturing of my boyish fancy began to rise in my mind and Robin Hood and his men to stand before me. The horn of Robin Hood again seemed to resound through the forest. I saw in this sylvan scenery half huntsmen, half freebooters, trooping across the distant glades or feasting and revelling beneath the trees.'

Local author and historian, William Howitt (born at Heanor in 1792) was also captivated by the splendour of Sherwood Forest and wrote:'A thousand years, ten thousand tempests, lightnings, winds and wintry violence have all flung their utmost force on these trees and there they stand, trunk after trunk, scathed, hollow, grey, gnarled; stretching out their bare, sturdy arms or their mingled foliage and ruin – a life in death. All is grey and old. The ground is grey beneath. The trees are grey with clinging lichens and the heather and ferns that spring up beneath have a character of the past. You stand and look around and in the height of summer all is silent; it is like the fragment of a world worn out and forsaken. These were the trees under which King John pursued the red deer. These were the oaks under which Robin Hood led up his bold band of outlaws. These are the oaks which have stood while king after king have resigned, while countries have flourished and decayed, dynasties have come and gone, while revolution after revolution and war after war have devastated and changed the face of the world. Amid all these vast changes, these mighty forest trees have been growing in grandeur and maturing in age until now, as we behold them they present a spectacle majestic almost beyond conception.'

Several of Sherwood's ancient oaks have their own legendary tales, such as the Parliament Oak, which was situated about 2 miles from Clipstone. The tree acquired its name after Edward I apparently held a parliament beneath its branches in 1290. King John is also believed to have summoned a council of his barons under this tree to convince them to sanction the immediate execution of 28 Welsh hostages (mostly children) who were imprisoned at Nottingham Castle. In fact, the king personally rode over to Nottingham to see that his brutal command was satisfactorily obeyed, then returned to Clipstone to continue his hunting! Sadly, over the centuries the trunk of this historic tree gradually decayed, leaving the pieces to rot on the forest floor!

Robin Hood's Larder was the name given to another of Sherwood's old oaks where tradition claims that the famous outlaw used to hang haunches of venison from its branches. Having survived being set on fire many years ago, its charred and hollow trunk were eventually blown down in a fierce gale in 1962! Half a mile from Welbeck Abbey once stood the Greendale Oak, a giant of a tree with a girth that measured some forty feet around its base and in 1724 a coach road was made through the oak by creating an opening six foot three inches wide and ten foot three inches high. The traditional story says that the 'archway' through the tree resulted from an after-dinner bet by Henry, the first Duke of Portland, who boasted that there was a tree in his park through which he could drive a coach and four and in 1727, artist George Vertue made an etching that depicted a carriage of that period, with six horses, being driven through the tree!

Quite apart from the sheer size and age of the ancient oaks of Sherwood Forest, oak trees in general were regarded in forest folklore as traditionally possessing mystical powers of prophecy and healing. The most famous oak 'oracle tree', known for its ability to foretell the future, grew at Dodona in north-west Greece and was believed to have been sacred to Zeus. Legend says that a branch from the tree was incorporated in the construction of the Argo, the vessel sailed in by Jason and the Argonauts on their quest for the Golden Fleece and warnings from the branch kept the crew safe during their journey.

Ancient beliefs often maintained that trees were inhabited by gods and oaks were known as 'thunder-trees', once sacred to the Norse god, Thor and were thought to protect against lightning and thunderbolts! Anyone sheltering under its branches during a storm was considered to be safe. Oak leaves were also worn to protect against witchcraft and evil and some country superstitions believe that when an oak tree is felled it gives a kind of shriek and groan that may be heard a mile off! To carry an acorn around as a charm helped preserve youthfulness and if an oak was struck by lightning the wood was said to gain additional protective powers, so folk would keep pieces inside their dwellings to prevent their homes suffering from a similar misfortune.

SHERWOOD FOREST...
TEXAS!

A t first glance, the idea of creating a medieval style Sherwood Forest in Texas, USA may seem to be a somewhat bizarre and far-fetched proposal but, 4 years ago, two former graduates of Texas A and M University did exactly that and on February 27th 2010, the "Sherwood Forest Faire" opened on Saturdays and Sundays for six consecutive weekends, offering a mixture of medieval entertainment and fun for the whole family! The concept was the brainchild of Eric Todd, a medieval and renaissance history graduate at the University who had visited Nottingham when he was a student 20 years earlier and had since tirelessly pursued his dream to build a piece of medieval Nottingham in the heart of Texas!

To achieve his goal, Eric and his business partner George Appling had to work really hard to secure the investment of 2.5 million dollars needed to acquire land in a suitable location and to turn the idea into a reality. They purchased a 106 acre forest site in an area known as "Lost Pines", (a stretch of land situated some 35 -45 miles east of Austin, the state capital, which has a huge stand of loblolly pine trees that offer good year-round shade) and set about creating the right ambience and entertainment facilities to establish the new attraction as a "must-see" Medieval Renaissance Park with a wide popular appeal.

Just two years later, in 2012, the Faire had grown significantly featuring over 100 live performances per day ; great food and various fun rides etc. and the 2014 event had over 130 merchant stalls and "shoppes", plus 40 stage acts scheduled , all helping to keep Austin "the Live Music Capital of the Nation"! To help ensure the venue's future viability, the owners also introduced an extended range of new initiatives that used the facilities at other times of the year, beyond the Annual Faire schedule. These included running Summer Camps, holding a Celtic Music Festival, offering wedding and banqueting facilities and staging Full Contact Jousting tournaments. Quite an achievement from a "standing start"!

Now, in comparison, let's take a look at the development record of the Visitor Centre at Nottinghamshire's "real" Sherwood Forest, that officially opened to the public in 1976 and consisted of a number of octagonal buildings called "pods" which housed a Robin Hood /Sherwood Forest display and exhibition; a small lecture theatre; a souvenir and gift shop and the Rangers offices. In addition there was a cafeteria/restaurant and a small tourist information centre. The events, walks and attractions on offer generally focus on the Forest's flora and fauna and the conservation and protection of the environment as a natural habitat. Thirty years ago this summer, the Visitor Centre staged the very first Robin Hood Festival that successfully grew to become an annual feature steadily building on its visitor numbers with 50,000 attending the free 7 day event in 2013.

In 2018, the RSPB (Royal Society For The Protection of Birds) formed a consortium to look after the site and in 2018 a new Visitor Centre was officially opened that signalled the beginning of a new era for the future management of Sherwood Forest.

So what are the lessons that the County authorities can learn from their Texan counterparts?

Clearly there are many distinct differences and complex issues between the nature and approach to the two forest projects that make direct comparison difficult but there are also some common factors that might raise a few eyebrows when you consider the widely contrasting timescales! Securing private sector investment and sponsorship is obviously a key issue but the most notable difference would seem to be the fact that the developers of the Texas Sherwood Forest simply just "got on with it" and, from a standing start, achieved their goal in just 2-3 years - whereas the Nottinghamshire Sherwood Forest project seemed to have been plagued by delays and issues that stretched back well over a decade!

SOCIAL JUSTICE

I am sure there have been many individuals throughout history who, in one form or another, adopted the practice of 'robbing the rich to give to the poor'. However, across the ages, this particular virtue seems to have become permanently entwined with the development of the traditional Robin Hood legend; and it has established itself in the hearts and minds of the public as probably the outlaw folk hero's most endearing principle. There are many examples of fair play and social justice that surround the traditional character of Robin Hood, and no doubt these are one of the key reasons for the outlaw's timeless popularity. 'Robbing the rich to give to the poor' reflects history's recurring theme of the eternal battle between the 'have's' and the 'have-not's', and even over the last couple of decades or so contemporary exponents of this practice have been referred to as 'modern-day Robin Hoods'.

*For example, the people of Thailand who go to work in other countries and send money back home are called 'Robin Hooders', and the terminology has also been adopted by other immigrant communities who follow the practice.

*In the Romanian capital of Bucharest, the charity CRY (Care and Relief for the Young) established their Casa Robin Hood project and opened an orphanage that through the symbolism of its name reflected the famous outlaw's association with the principles of caring for the poor.

*Guitar superstar Eric Clapton described the concept for his Crossroads Centre addiction and rehabilitation project in Antigua as being "a Robin Hood scheme really, whereby drawing on people from America and Europe who would pay to come there, it funded scholarship beds for the locals who couldn't afford it."

*New York City's Robin Hood Foundation was set-up in 1988 by multi-millionaire stockbroker and philanthropist, Paul Tudor Jones and its philosophy uses business techniques and financial guidance, instead of just giving donations to charities and community groups and letting them get on with it. The organisation stated that "the idea of helping the poor is inextricably linked to Robin Hood and the founders knew that it was the ideal image for the foundation". It has given out over £80m – all in the name of Nottinghamshire's own folk hero!

*Top-flight litigation lawyer, Stephen Alexander was so boastful of his devotion to the cause of victims of injustice (especially when they suffered at the hands of giant companies or governments) that he commissioned a poster of himself pictured like Kevin Costner in the 'Robin Hood – Prince of Thieves' movie!

However, there are instances where giving someone the 'Robin Hood' title gets carried a bit too far. American financial consultant Allen Klein was known as 'the Robin Hood of Pop' through his reputation for recouping millions of dollars for his clients from seemingly iron-clad record company percentages; he acted for the likes of the Rolling Stones, the Beatles, and the Kinks, not necessarily many people's idea of 'giving to the poor'! And just weeks ago music industry boss Duncan Schwier, 52, was described as a 'Robin Hood' after stealing nearly £650,000 from the record label Universal Music Group, spending £400,000 on staff bonuses, parties and gifts, as well as giving £100,000 to charity. He was jailed for three years after admitted theft from his employer – ironically, he was caught out when he was given a promotion and his successor discovered invoices to bogus companies.

The Robin Hood Tax was devised as an initiative potentially capable of turning a crisis for the banks into "an opportunity for the world" – and probably represents one of the most high-profile recent international examples of the use of the Robin Hood name which clearly reflects his own style of social justice. Bringing together the support of nearly 60 organisations, including Oxfam, the TUC, Barnardos, ActionAid, the Salvation Army and Save The Children, the proposed 0.05% tax would be levied on financial services companies for transactions like stocks, bonds, and foreign currency and derivatives.

The organisers say which could raise £250 billion a year globally, which would then be used to combat poverty, famine, protect public services and help make the world a better place. In the UK alone it is predicted that it would bring in £20 billion annually. The Robin Hood Tax campaign group says: "The Robin Hood Tax is justice. The banks can afford it. The systems are in place to collect it. It won't affect ordinary members of the public, their bank accounts or their savings. It's fair, it's timely, and it's possible." The proposal is similar to the previously suggested Tobin

Tax, although that was originally intended to be aimed solely at currency exchanges.

Since the idea of the Robin Hood Tax was launched in 2010, more than 750,000 people have backed it so far. But while European finance ministers have agreed to take action on some financial transactions, this falls short of the full Robin Hood Tax which has been proposed.

A FEATHER IN THE CAP

There are many types of recognisable headgear that instantly identify the group the wearer belongs to - including the cowboy's stetson, the knight's armoured helmet, the pirate's bandana, the fireman's hard-hat and the American Indian's head-dress etc. - but the one item of headwear that immediately establishes an association with a single person's name is the traditional Robin Hood Hat!

The familiar, triangular-shaped cloth cap with a feather in it has become an iconic and recognisable item of clothing that universally identifies the wearer as "Robin Hood"! Historians tell us that it was probably originally designed as a practical piece of medieval headgear used primarily by foresters, as its slim forward-pointing brim avoided it catching the string of their longbows when firing an arrow. The simplicity of the style, with some decorative additions, later saw the hat evolve into the mainstream fashion of the period. The familiar shaped hat has also been used as the distinguishing feature on numerous illustrations and commercial brands ranging from the giant US Walmart supermarket chain to, at a more local level, "The Nottingham" building society and it is frequently worn by campaigners for social justice such as Oxfam's Robin

Hood Tax initiative and representative groups such as the California Nurses Association.

One of the most famous uses of the hat "brand" is by the Robin Hood Flour Company based in Saskatchewan, Canada, who first introduced it on their stylised logo when the business was founded in 1909. In fact, the flour brand became so well known as a household name in North America that the original logo was actually used as the reference that inspired Errol Flynn's iconic hat and costume for Warner Brothers classic 1938 movie "The Adventures of Robin Hood".

Another, somewhat unusual, Hollywood connection was recounted by film star, Katharine Hepburn in her memoirs of the making of the 1951, Oscar nominated movie, "The African Queen." She recalls being on location in Uganda, South Africa and on a break from filming, accompanying her co-star, Humphrey Bogart and director, John Huston on an expedition into the bush. Describing the party setting-off, she states, "We were walking along in single file, each one carrying his own things. We were led by the black native that knew this country. He carried a sort of spear about six or seven feet long. He was naked except for a pair of vey short shorts and he wore a dark-green Robin Hood hat, pointed in crown and in brim."

There are of course literally hundreds of pubs, inns and hotels with Robin Hood related names and on the pictorial signs that usually hang outside these establishments, Robin is frequently shown wearing the characteristic hat with a feather and, on some of the older signs, the artists often disproportionately over-emphasised the size of the feather, making the hat look more like a cavalier's headwear from the English Civil War!

Over the centuries that the Robin Hood tales have been told and re-told, the Robin Hood Hat has been the simplest of costumes by which to define the character and has become an essential stock wardrobe item in schools, amateur dramatic productions and theatre and repertory companies. Easy to make and store - yet instantly recognisable.

It has also proved indispensable to cartoonists who found that by just adding a simply drawn Robin Hood hat to their illustrations the figures quickly conveyed the context of the character they were trying to create. So whether they were a political satirist depicting David Cameron as the "Sheriff of Notting Hill" or Mickey Mouse, Tom and Jerry or Bugs Bunny on a Sherwood Forest caper in an animated film short, showing them wearing a Robin Hood hat with feather immediately put their drawings in character.

However, not everyone saw the traditional hat in an attractive light. To some it seemed twee and hackneyed and (excuse the pun!) old hat and a look-back at a few of the more recent portrayals of Robin Hood on the big and small screen shows that Russell Crowe, Kevin Costner, Patrick Bergin, Michael Praed and Jonas Armstrong preferred to ditch the iconic Errol Flynn headgear as being out-dated and old-fashioned. Perhaps they felt it was not masculine enough for a hard-hitting, modern day film hero and so their costumes incorporated the use of a hood or cowl, more in keeping with the outlaw's name and ability to slip un-recognised into the safety of Sherwood Forest.

But the Robin Hood hat still remains a firm favourite with the general public ; a fact that is confirmed by its popularity as a top-selling visitor souvenir and fancy dress costume. So, whether it's young boys wearing one to act out their hero in a wooden sword fight or "big boys" with one jauntily perched on their heads on a Nottingham Stag Night, the Robin Hood hat still survives and is here to stay!

The most essential and recognisable feature of a traditional Robin Hood hat is, of course, the feather and the origins of this symbolic decoration lie in a general world-wide custom adopted by hunters and warriors. The forester who killed his first game-bird signified the honour of his achievement by putting a single feather in his cap, just as the American Indians added a feather to their head dress for every enemy slain and many other tribes and civilisations throughout history had similar practices.

NATIONAL TREASURES!

I n the glitzy world of today's celebrity culture, the term "National Treasure" is sometimes too freely attributed to people who do not really have the longevity or profile to deserve such an accolade!

However, Robin Hood has been frequently referred to in these terms and is not just a "national treasure" but is also globally recognised as the world's favourite adventure hero, whose 800 year old story is a legendary classic!

So I got to wondering if other countries also regarded their folk heroes as "National Treasures" - and if and how they used these iconic figures to promote their country to the international tourism industry etc.? That's when I came across a report on how Transylvania markets its Count Dracula legend and realised that Nottingham and Nottinghamshire may be only playing in the minor league!

An article from the professional business magazine "Marketing" outlined how the Transylvanian government had secured a European Council funded programme to develop a strategy for Romania's huge tourist potential and had identified Dracula as a separate national tourist asset, alongside Black Sea beaches, mountains and spas. This had brought about a World Dracula Congress in Bucharest in 1995 attended by historians, folklorists and "vampir-ologists" from all around the globe.

Recognising the value of an international brand name such as Dracula, the Transylvanian Society of Dracula had established itself as a non-profit making organisation and to fund its activities, it offered Dracula Tours, ranging from a Grade One Tour - "suitable for balanced, classical minds, interested in the Gothic approaches to issues of broader existence" - to Grade Three tours, reserved for true initiates!

The organisation also produced a collection of quality merchandise aimed at tourists that encompassed the finest Romania had to offer in silverware, glass, and china etc. – all discreetly hallmarked with the Dracula logo –a dragon in the shape of the letter D!"

From a completely opposite marketing perspective, I later read about the tiny community of Hell, in southeast Michigan, USA, that uses all the benefits of its iconic name with the obvious word-play on "going to Hell" or "going through Hell" etc. A convenience store and bait shop also served as the Post Office, where you could get letters hand-stamped with a "From Hell" postmark or a message to let the world know that you've "been to Hell and back!" They even sold tiny baseball bats engraved with "A Bat out of Hell!"

Whatever you might think of these two extremely different approaches, in their own way, they both make the absolute most of their legendary associations – which is a conundrum that Nottingham City and County are still struggling with!

STYLE ICON?

I wonder how many people realise that our ubiquitous folk hero, Robin Hood, also knows how to set trends in the style and costume business – and it's not just down to him wearing green tights!

In 1938, when the classic Errol Flynn movie "The Adventures of Robin Hood" was breaking box office records and receiving Oscar nominations, Hollywood's fashion conscious designers were quick to adapt the influences of the iconic Robin Hood hat into stylish millinery that tastefully complimented the tailored suits and smart dresses being paraded on the catwalks. Originally used by Medieval foresters as practical, working headgear, the traditional features of the hooded cowl and the long pointed brim with decorative feather were innovatively interpreted into fashionable feminine hats and hoods that appeared in numerous films of the era and often also became a focal point of consumer advertising in magazines and on billboards. (One of the most famous designs was used to promote the Craven A brand of cigarettes in a perfect blend of taste and style!).

In more recent times the Robin Hood "brand" was even developed by Far Eastern fashion entrepreneurs into the Robin Hood of China casual clothing range, featuring jeans, sweaters, jackets and leisure wear accessories that carried the image of Robin shooting an arrow as the trademark embroidered logo.

Apart from always being in the Top Ten designs for fancy dress (hired or homemade!), Robin is also a popular theme in the world of canine couture! That's right – dressing up your pet pooch is a passion with certain sectors of America's doggy-doting community and among the selection of themed apparel for dogs on the internet is – you guessed it – the obligatory Robin Hood outfit!

It seems that even now, many centuries after their Medieval origins, hats, hoods (and tights) can still set the fashion!

CHRISTMAS ROBINS!

So what on earth has Robin Hood got to do with Christmas? Well, surprisingly, the outlaw hero's legendary status in global popular culture has developed some strong links with the traditional festive season.

Of course, Christmas is also the time for the traditional British pantomime and it was way back in 1867 that the storyline of the popular panto, 'Babes in the Wood' first introduced the character of Robin Hood and Victorian audiences and critics were somewhat bemused by his sudden appearance! Based on an old English ballad of 1595, the story of two children abandoned deep in the forest by their wicked uncle, was originally first staged as an opera at the Haymarket Theatre in 1798 and called 'The Children in the Wood'. However, it would be over 30 years later, in 1827 before the first 'pantomime' version of the story was presented at Drury Lane under the title of 'The Babes in the Wood'.

A glance at Robin Hood's "historical" timeline clearly shows that he reputedly lived well over 200 years before the story of the Babes in the Wood was created but after he first appeared in the 1867 production at Covent Garden, Robin quickly became established into the pantomime version along with his Merry Men (who were all played by women) and Maid Marian, who became the nurse to the babes. Literary historians believe that introducing Robin Hood and his companions into the drama was a significant and successful move, as this second story line was one already known to children and helped expand the somewhat weak main plot to help guarantee its popularity with family audiences, often resulting in Robin getting headline billing with productions being frequently called 'Robin Hood and the Babes in the Wood'. Ironically, Robin had already been the subject of his 'own' pantomime, since 'Merry Sherwood' in the 1790's, so his unexpected and unlikely appearance in the Babes in the Wood proved to be somewhat baffling. In fact, as late as 1888, the Times newspaper continued to express surprise at Robin Hood's association with the production stating that 'the babes were mixed up with the proceedings of Robin Hood and his Merry Men in Sherwood Forest owing to the accidental circumstance, as it would seem, of Maid Marian having been engaged as their governess.'

Aspects of the traditional Robin Hood legend soon made their mark on various versions of the 'Babes in the Wood' pantomime and in Act Two, the children are guided to Robin Hood's encampment in Sherwood Forest and the storyline also often includes a scene at Nottingham Goose Fair and an archery contest. The pantomime's conclusion sees the babes return to Nottingham Castle and the villainous Sheriff/Wicked Uncle defeated. The children claim their rightful inheritance and are subsequently looked after by Robin and Marian, who usually marry at the end of the Act, prompting lots of emotional sighs from the audience!

Some historians hold the view that Robin Hood's real roots are entwined with the mystical beliefs of ancient English folklore, so it perhaps comes as no surprise to learn that one theory suggests that, in a similar way to how he is often connected to the Green Man, Nottingham's famous outlaw may have also evolved through traditional links to the robin, the friendly, red-breasted garden bird whose image features so prominently on thousands of seasonal greetings cards. In 2012, author, journalist and etymologist Steve Moxon focussed on the close relationship between the two Robins (Hood and Redbreast) and stated 'Given that we have more of a concrete handle on the bird robin than on Robin Hood, then this seems like a good starting point to attack the mystery but the problem is that there isn't an etymology (how the word was derived) even for the bird!' However, to avoid taking readers through the complexity of the various viewpoints and their often relatively inconclusive findings I will sum up the issue in the following simple terms. The robin is referred to in folklore as 'the oak king' and in the context of the traditional year-end (St Stephen's Day – Boxing Day) the processional ritual of 'hunting the wren' takes place and uses the sympathetic magic of regeneration mythology to ensure the resumption of life and fertility, which are seemingly gone forever with the onset of Winter. It is a supposed battle between 'the oak king' of the new year (the robin) and 'the holly king' of the old year (the wren) that gave rise to the barbaric practised custom where a group of men take up on behalf of the robin to seek and kill a wren and parade the body about the village. Not surprisingly, Steve Moxon comments 'The curious aspect of this is that although in context the two birds were considered 'kings' – so both were considered as male – they were also imagined as husband and wife, the robin as male and the wren female!' Apparently, this is how we got the terms 'cock robin' and 'jenny wren'! How confusing is that!

Of course we are all familiar with seeing images of the robin on our Christmas cards but in recent years I have noticed that one or two designs have sometimes shown the robin wearing a jaunty green Robin Hood hat and even carrying a bow, so that loose word association with the two robins (bird and outlaw) still exists!

Christmas is also a time for great feasting and merry making so one might have expected to find a more specific reference in the Robin Hood ballads and traditional stories to the events of the festive season but there is hardly anything of significance. Perhaps it's because Robin and his band were generally well provided for in their Sherwood Forest encampment and regularly used any excuse to break out the food and drink for a celebration whenever they had a 'guest' or had completed a successful adventure. No doubt the troubadours and players who travelled around the country would also regularly embellish their stories from the Robin Hood legend with topical, seasonal references for their performances in castles, manor houses, taverns and market places etc. but it appears that these variations were never significant enough to become permanently adapted into any of the traditional Robin Hood tales.

However, it was probably a more recent contemporary dramatisation of the Robin Hood legend that brought Christmas back into the story when, in Kevin Costner's blockbuster movie, 'Robin Hood: Prince of Thieves', actor Alan Rickman's scene-stealing performance, playing the evil Sheriff of Nottingham in a fit of rage because things were not going his way, delivered the classic line 'That's it then! Cancel the kitchen scraps for lepers and orphans, no more merciful beheadings and Call off Christmas!' – creating a phrase which ultimately found its way into movie history's popular culture!

HE'S BEHIND YOU ...AND HE'S EVERYWHERE!

Whenever the festive pantomime season approaches, I'm reminded how, over recent years, our local folk hero, Robin Hood has worked his way from being a minor role in a traditional panto to the "star billing" he now gets in the many latter-day productions that are re-titled "Robin Hood and the Babes in the Wood"!

For centuries, numerous alehouses and hostelries, along with countless geographical locations and landmarks, have been given a Robin Hood related name and, in its way, this represents the origins of one of the earliest forms of what in today's commercial and marketing "savvy" world is known as "branding"!

Popular culture has always eagerly clamoured to seek out ways to become associated with the world famous legend and you have only to look at the vast range of books, plays, poems, films and television scripts etc. to see that creative writers of all genres have frequently stepped up to ride the "Robin Hood Merry Go Round" for inspiration, because they know that

Robin's reputation as "the people's hero" still strikes an enduring chord with the global public.

In fact, surprisingly, there have also been several other high profile ventures under consideration that for one reason or another did not materialise and became "the Robin Hood's that never were"!

When "Jesus Christ Superstar" first struggled to make an impact, Andrew Lloyd Webber and Tim Rice were quoted as saying "Back to the drawing board - let's do one on Robin Hood!"

Hugh Grant and Liz Hurley also planned to star as Robin and Marian and secured the options on a rom-com script provisionally titled "Bows and Arrows" and Rupert Wainwright (director of the much-acclaimed 1999 movie "Stigmata") also bought the rights to a horror-style interpretation of the Robin Hood story called "Blood of Sherwood" but the film has yet to be made!

Towards the end of their career, iconic comedy duo, Laurel and Hardy, also considered making a comic film version of the popular Robin Hood story but the project never materialised!

Although, Robin Hood was around long before the term "a global icon" was created, the internationally renowned folk hero has become just that. A world-wide superstar! In fact, it seems that barely a year goes by without talk of a new film, book or revelation about the Sherwood outlaw and references to him are made in the global media on an almost daily basis. **A true testimony of how the legacy of the Robin Hood legend continues to live on!**

RECOMMENDED READING

In around 1489, *"A Lytell Geste of Robyn Hoode"* became the first published collection of ballads to be printed about the famous outlaw and since that time thousands of Robin Hood books have been written over the centuries. The World Wide Robin Hood Society is often asked by students by and enthusiasts to recommend books to read, so here is a very brief, personal selection – followed by my reviews of two fairly recent publications that look at the Robin Hood legend from two different perspectives.

Traditional Classics: *"Robin Hood and the Men of the Greenwood"* by Henry Gilbert – plus any of the superbly illustrated books by Howard Pyle or Louis Rhead.

Historic/Academic/Factual: Richard Rutherford-Moore's *"The Legend of Robin Hood"* succinctly puts the stories into a local context, as does Jim Lees' *"The Quest for Robin Hood."* For a more serious academic analysis, try Prof. Stephen Knight's *"Robin Hood – A mythic biography"* or A.J. Pollard's *"Imagining Robin Hood – The Late-Medieval Stories in Historical Context".*

Children's Books: My personal favourites are *"Robin Hood"* by David Calcutt with magnificent illustrations by award-winning Grahame Baker-Smith: the prize-winning modern morality tale *"The Sherwood Hero"* by Alison Prince and *"The Tunnellers" (Maid Marion's People)* " by local Nottinghamshire author, Helen Dennis.

Film and Television associated: Any of Richard Carpenter's books linked to the 1980's HTV series "Robin of Sherwood" – my particular favourite is *"The Swords of Wayland"*.

Poems and Ballads: For a comprehensive view on the medieval ballads, plus lots of background information, try *"The Robin Hood Handbook"* by Mike Kennedy-Dixon.

Romantic Fiction: *"The Arrow of Sherwood"* by Lauren Johnson, offers a plausible blend of historical fact and fiction in this period drama of the Robin Hood tale.

Humorous Spoofs: *"Robin Hood according to Spike Milligan"* is a zany rendition that reflects a quirky sense of humour and for an even more light-hearted connection try Tony Robinson's *"Maid Marian and her Merry Men"* books from the popular children's TV series.

Science Fiction: *"Arrowhead"*, an apocalyptic version by Paul Kane: or *"Erasmus Hobart and the Golden Arrow"* by local Nottinghamshire author, Andrew Fish, which links the legend to a time traveler with a medieval twist!

Comic Strips: Respected graphic artist, Frank Bellamy's *"Robin Hood – the complete adventures"*, brings together his classic series that appeared in the Swift comic during the 1950's.

Novelty and miscellaneous: *"Robin Hood"* a touch-n-listen version for children by Golden Books of New York features audio sounds (powered by a cell battery in the cover) that can be added to the story where indicated in the text; *"Robin Hood & Friar Tuck – Zombie Killers"* by Paul A. Freeman is a clever and fascinating narrative poem written in the style of Geoffery Chaucer's Canterbury Tales. Kevin Carpenter's *"Robin Hood – The Many Faces of that Celebrated English Outlaw"* is actually a comprehensive catalogue of the fascinating Robin Hood - related items displayed in a 1995 exhibition but it provides a wonderful insight into the impact that Robin Hood has had on the development of popular culture. *"Robin The Hoodie – An ASBO History of Britain"* by Hans Christian Asbosen is described as being "painstakingly mistranslated from the original sources and a treasury of anti-social tales from history that will help you forget all that nonsense they taught you at school." It is also the only Robin Hood book that I have ever come across that has "Warning: Adults Only. Not Suitable For Children" printed on the back cover!

Finally here are my reviews of the two books I mentioned earlier that look at the Robin Hood legend from differing viewpoints!

'The Life and Times of the Real Robyn Hoode' by Mark Olly: With no proven, undisputed historical evidence being available as to who Robin Hood actually was, the 'man or myth' conundrum has continued to be a mystery that has fascinated generation after generation and turned the English folklore hero into an iconic global legend. Consequently, there are numerous speculative and plausible theories about his existence, lineage, birthplace and burial site etc. to keep academics and enthusiasts occupied for years to come or until there is an extremely unlikely 'Richard III moment' when someone discovers a DNA linked skeleton!

In the meantime, historians and individuals fastidiously comb through centuries of manuscripts and medieval records to try to piece together the intriguing puzzle that is further complicated by a blurring of the historic fact and the development and fusing of the tales into traditional folklore legend. In fact, it is often said that Robin Hood has become a million times richer as an icon of popular culture than as a genuine historical figure!

Whatever your views and opinions, Mark Olly's *'The Life and Times of the Real Robyn Hoode'* is an excellent place to start.

Using literary archaeology, the author has logically brought together the historical background authenticated by existing material and records and produced a credible timeline into which the various aspects, characters and locations associated with the legend can be feasibly connected. His decision to place all the original source texts relating to the life of the real Robyn Hoode in **bold type** so it can be read as a complete separate narrative if desired and to show all the source manuscripts and quotes in Italics, also helps the reader to differentiate between the origins of the material.

Mark has deliberately avoided getting 'side-tracked' by the explosion of contemporary popular culture associated with the legend and perhaps the book's greatest achievement lies in the style of writing and presentation. Although it is packed with interesting, relevant information, this is not a 'stuffy' reference source and in its easy- to-read 202 pages Mark Olly has compactly set out the background for any interested readers to 'investigate' the complexity of the Robin Hood legend for themselves.

Over the years, I have read and reviewed many Robin Hood related books, both fact and fiction and in my opinion this is one of the best recent reference works on the subject.

(Bob White, Chairman, World Wide Robin Hood Society.)

'Why Everything You Know About Robin Hood Is Wrong' by Karen Murdarasi: Man or Myth – Fact or Fiction? The Robin Hood legend is actually a can of worms! The problem is that if you take a serious look into the background to the popular traditional tales you'll discover it's riddled with flaws. The facts often don't stack up and somehow it seems impossible to square the circle between the story and the reality. That's the obsessive nature of the legend that has continued to fascinate and infuriate academics and enthusiasts for centuries.

With the no-nonsense, cover title of 'Why Everything You Know About Robin Hood Is Wrong' – Karen Murdarasi's new book pulls no punches and tells it like it is! The 90 informative pages are jam-packed with revealing facts and comparisons about the many discrepancies in the popular story and it's all brightly written in a succinct and engaging style. The author outlines some of the main issues that have caused controversy and debate in academic circles and puts forward five possible pretenders from the lengthy list of 'usual suspects' championed by various historians, all suggesting real life characters who Robin Hood may have been based on.

There is no undisputed historical evidence available that can conclusively prove that Robin Hood ever existed or who he really was. However, across the centuries, fiction has triumphed over fact and Robin Hood has become far more significant as a legend than ever he would have been as a real historical figure.

Every generation creates for itself the Robin Hood that it needs and the public have always come to his rescue whenever his credibility is called into question. Irrespective of any new supposed facts or information to the contrary, Robin Hood is the

People's Champion , a global icon of popular culture and the general public have repeatedly shown that they do not wish the image of their legendary Sherwood Forest hero, and everything he stands for, to be destroyed. However, if your curiosity gets the better of you and you really want to delve into the murky world of Robin Hood's authenticity, then Karen Murdarasi spells it all out in this enjoyable new book.

.

Hour of the Jackals
By Emil Eugensen

Soft Hunger
By Lucrezia Brambillaschi

Robin Hood: The Legacy of a Folk Hero
By Robert White

I Am This Girl: Tales of Youth
By Samantha Benjaminn

Arthur: Shadow of a God
By Richard Denham

Dark and Light Tales of Ripton Town
By John Decarteret

Mixed Rhythms and Shady Rhymes
By Teresa Fowler

Thin Blue Rhymes
By various authors

Click Bait
By Gillian Philip

The Woe of Roanoke
By Mathew Horton

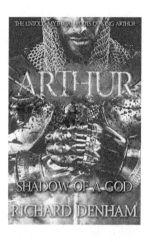

Arthur: Shadow of a God
By Richard Denham

King Arthur has fascinated the Western world for over a thousand years and yet we still know nothing more about him now than we did then. Layer upon layer of heroics and exploits has been piled upon him to the point where history, legend and myth have become hopelessly entangled.

In recent years, there has been a sort of scholarly consensus that 'the once and future king' was clearly some sort of Romano-British warlord, heroically stemming the tide of wave after wave of Saxon invaders after the end of Roman rule. But surprisingly, and no matter how much we enjoy this narrative, there is actually next-to-nothing solid to support this theory except the wishful thinking of understandably bitter contemporaries. The sources and scholarship used to support the 'real Arthur' are as much tentative guesswork and pushing 'evidence' to the extreme to fit in with this version as anything involving magic swords, wizards and dragons. Even Archaeology remains silent. Arthur is, and always has been, the square peg that refuses to fit neatly into the historians round hole.

Arthur: Shadow of a God gives a fascinating overview of Britain's lost hero and casts a light over an often-overlooked and somewhat inconvenient truth; Arthur was almost certainly not a man at all, but a god. He is linked inextricably to the world of Celtic folklore and Druidic traditions. Whereas tyrants like Nero and Caligula were men who fancied themselves gods; is it not possible that Arthur was a god we have turned into a man? Perhaps then there is a truth here. Arthur, 'The King under the Mountain'; sleeping until his return will never return, after all, because he doesn't need to. Arthur the god never left in the first place and remains as popular today as he ever was. His legend echoes in stories, films and games that are every bit as imaginative and fanciful as that which the minds of talented bards such as Taliesin and Aneirin came up with when the mists of the 'dark ages' still swirled over Britain – and perhaps that is a good thing after all, most at home in the imaginations of children and adults alike – being the Arthur his believers want him to be.

Fade
By Bethan White

Do you want to remember?

Do you want to forget?

There is nothing extraordinary about Chris Rowan. Each day he wakes to the same faces, has the same breakfast, the same commute, the same sort of homes he tries to rent out to unsuspecting tenants.

There is nothing extraordinary about Chris Rowan. That is apart from the black dog that haunts his nightmares and an unexpected encounter with a long forgotten demon from his past. A nudge that will send Chris on his own downward spiral, from which there may be no escape.

There is nothing extraordinary about Chris Rowan...

Hour of the Jackals
By Emil Eugensen

It is a time of chaos, a time of vengeance, an hour of jackals.

A shadow stirs. Why is the US president slowly losing his mind? Why is Europe falling apart and why are fascist coups seemingly imminent across the world?

A Chinese spy and his American colleague try to deduce who is behind everything. An English professor makes a Faustian deal to get revenge on his daughter's racist attackers. A young federal agent falls in love with the woman he is ordered to betray. All the while the fascist conspirators are preparing their secret mind-control weapons.

Yet other, possibly supernatural, forces could be at play as well. Including one unearthly Domina, who will provide any information you may seek, but the payment is harsh indeed...

Click Bait
By Gillian Philip

A funny joke's a funny joke. Eddie Doolan doesn't think twice about adapting it to fit a tragic local news story and posting it on social media.

It's less of a joke when his drunken post goes viral. It stops being funny altogether when Eddie ends up jobless, friendless and ostracised by the whole town of Langburn. This isn't how he wanted to achieve fame.

Eddie knows he's blown his relationship with rich girl Lily Cumnock. It's Lily's possessive and controlling father Brodie who fires him from his job - and makes sure he won't find another decent one in Langburn. And Eddie doesn't even have Flo to fall back on - his old nan died some six months ago, and Eddie is still recovering from the death of the woman who raised him and who loved him unconditionally.

Under siege from the press, and facing charges not just for the joke but for a history of abusive behaviour on the internet, Eddie grows increasingly paranoid and desperate. The only people still speaking to him are Crow, a neglected kid who relies on Eddie for food and company, and Sid, the local gamekeeper's granddaughter. It's Sid who offers Eddie a refuge and an understanding ear.

But she also offers him an illegal shotgun - and as Eddie's life spirals downwards, and his efforts at redemption are thwarted at every turn, the gun starts to look like the answer to all his problems.

www.blkdogpublishing.com

Made in the USA
Coppell, TX
30 January 2021